DEAR JELAINE,

HAPPY MOTHERS DAY 2009!

LOVE, PAPA

A MOTHER'S BOOK OF SECRETS

A MOTHER'S BOOK OF SECRETS

LINDA EYRE AND
SHAWNI EYRE POTHIER

PHOTOGRAPHY BY SHAWNI EYRE POTHIER

DESERET
BOOK

SALT LAKE CITY, UTAH

Photograph on page xii courtesy Mark Mabry

Library of Congress Cataloging-in-Publication Data

Eyre, Linda.
    A mother's book of secrets / by Linda Eyre and Shawni Eyre Pothier.
        p.   cm.
    Includes bibliographical references.
    ISBN 978-1-60641-070-7 (hardbound : alk. paper)
  1. Mothers—Religious life.   2. Mormon women—Religious life.
3. Motherhood—Religious aspects—Church of Jesus Christ of Latter-day Saints.   4. Motherhood—Religious aspects—Mormon Church.   5. Child rearing—Religious aspects—Church of Jesus Christ of Latter-day Saints.
6. Child rearing—Religious aspects—Mormon Church.   I. Pothier, Shawni Eyre.   II. Title.
    BX8641.E97 2009
    242'.6431—dc22   2008037672

Printed in China
R. R. Donnelley and Sons, Shenzhen, China

10   9   8   7   6   5   4   3   2   1

CONTENTS

PART 4: KIDS ARE LIKE PUZZLES

PART 5: GIVE OWNERSHIP

INTRODUCTION

Linda

When people ask me if I *planned* to have nine children, I drop my head and admit that I didn't. They smile knowingly until I add, "Actually I planned to have *ten!*"

I know that sounds crazy, and certainly that route is not for everyone, but I knew from the get-go that I wanted to have a large, ultra-challenging, and exciting experience with parenthood!

By the time I graduated from college, I had found a remarkable guy who was brimming with great ideas about parenting—even though he was as strong-minded as I was, which definitely led to some lively disagreements. We moved to Boston on our honeymoon, and I taught school while Richard attended Harvard Business School. In my eighth month of pregnancy I "retired" and looked forward to the adventure of being a mother. I must admit that in the last moments of a crazy-horrendous, not-on-purpose natural childbirth, I secretly vowed *never* to enter the halls of a hospital for the purpose of childbirth again.

But the moment that beautiful little girl emerged from her world to ours and opened those misty baby eyes full of other-worldly wisdom and wonder, I knew that motherhood would be my most important career. As I thought about the challenge ahead of me, I anticipated a career that would be exciting and full of surprises and creativity. Little did I know just *how* creative I would have to be to survive. Nor did I have any inkling of how *many* surprises the coming years would hold!

In spite of that vow in the delivery room, I have indeed spent some more time at hospitals giving birth. With a lot of help from heaven, Richard and I have had the privilege of shepherding through life four daughters—Saren, Shawni, Saydi, and Charity—and five sons—Josh, Jonah, Talmadge, Noah, and Eli. We often say that we got one of every kind. Each sparkled with personality and complexity. They were perfect guinea pigs for our parenting ideas. And now, amazingly, those long years during which the halls of our home brimmed with love and joy, as well as "weeping and wailing," have passed. Six of our nine children are married, all are presently "on their own," and suddenly our children are having children—eighteen under twelve at this printing!

Richard and I have very much enjoyed writing books about what we have learned from our multifaceted children. And now, we have started writing books with those same children, who are definitely smarter than we are! For years, our second daughter, Shawni, and I had been talking about writing a book together. But until now, many issues held us up . . . mostly children . . . mine and hers! Shawni has an extraordinary passion for mothering. She and her husband, Dave, are the farthest along on their path of parenting among our children. She is the proud mother of five beautiful children, ages two to eleven, who you will come to know well as you read on.

Shawni is also an incredible photographer. Her passion for it shows, not only in the fabulous photographs of her own family but also in the moments of other families' joy that she captures through a lens. A picture is worth a thousand words, and we believe that photography, like music, can transport you into another realm of inspiration. We hope you feel that as you enjoy the moments of family life portrayed by Shawni in this book. Her gift for photography is equaled only by her ability to express her thoughts and feelings about motherhood straight from her passionate mother's heart. I am blessed to be her mother!

Together, Shawni and I are ready to share some secrets. We'll take turns letting you in on some of the things we've learned—or are still learning. Some will be secrets you already know and probably implement better than we do. Some will be short and sweet, others more instructive, but each is short enough to enjoy one small bite at a time. We hope, with the overall view of what I have learned through the whole spectrum of motherhood, along with Shawni's day-to-day, down and dirty—as well as delightful—mothering experiences, that what we have written will be a catalyst to developing your own secrets of success. (To share your secrets, see the postscript on page 156.)

As we explore these secrets together, no matter what your present circumstances are, may you remind yourselves that there isn't a more difficult yet more important and magnificent career than that of motherhood. In a world that is losing touch with the importance of motherhood, we think C. S. Lewis explained it best when he said, "[Motherhood and homemaking] is surely, in reality, the most important work in the world. What do ships, railways, mines, cars, government etc exist for except that people may be fed, warmed, and safe in their own homes? . . . [The homemaker's] job is the one for which all others exist" (*Collected Letters of C. S. Lewis,* 580).

INTRODUCTION

Shawni

It seems that I waited my whole life to be a mother. I was second of nine, and born with an abnormally passionate love of newborns (I think directly inherited from my amazing mother). I remember watching her in complete adoration (and a little bit of envy) as she got to bring home baby after baby from the hospital. Oh, how I loved those sweet babies, and how I longed with all my heart for one of my own. I'd "hoard" my brother and sister babies. I'd sneak in and hold them any chance I got. I would watch them sleep. I'd sit for hours studying their tiny hands and feet. I'd watch my mom in amazement as she allowed me and others to hold those sweet bundles. I'd wonder to myself about what would happen when I finally got my own babies . . . I was sure there was no way I'd ever be able to let others hold them. I'd be much too enamored with them to let anyone else have a turn.

Now here I am, in the thick of things, the mother of five of my very favorite people, trying to figure it all out as I go (and yes, I surprised myself and was actually OK with letting others hold them as babies). Although it didn't take long to realize that real motherhood is often very far from the picture-perfect dreams I had in mind when I was young, I wouldn't have it any other way. I'll take all the chaos and craziness because along with them come the moments I would not trade for the world.

Because you'll hear a lot about them in this book, my children need a brief introduction. Max is my oldest. He's eleven. He's tall, a little bit shy, and has the best slow smile that brightens up his whole face . . . just like his dad's. He's followed by four girls: Elle, who's ten and who's also tall (you'll notice a trend here), graceful, and very nurturing of all those around her. Grace is seven and is filled to the brim with spunk and strong-will. Claire is five and is very enthusiastic about life. She has bright, sparkly eyes inherited directly from her Nana. And then there's Lucy, our "baby," who's in the thick of the terrible twos. She has a few developmental delays, but she seems to be very advanced in the skill of throwing a good tantrum.

Sometimes I feel like I could conquer the world and that I've got motherhood all figured out. But most times I'm barely hanging on by my fingernails. I think that's how motherhood is. We get suckered into so much chaos that we sometimes forget to enjoy the journey. And before we know it, that journey with small children will be gone . . . nothing but a faded memory.

That's why my mom and I wanted to write down some of the things we've learned along the way—some of the "secrets" that have helped us through the trenches of motherhood. I couldn't be more excited to get to write a book about something I'm so passionate about and to do it at the side of a woman who I think is one of the most amazing examples of all: my mother. She raised nine children as individuals. She somehow knew instinctively all the secrets we cover in this book. She made motherhood her career and did an exceptional job at it.

Some of these secrets will be old hat to you. You'll have them down. Some will be new. But it's always invigorating to think through things over and over again. Even something you have down pat can be built upon when given more thought and attention. Motherhood is something that must be made and re-made and re-made. Each new re-make builds on the last and makes motherhood even more rewarding.

We wish you much joy and happiness in your motherhood career. May we learn to love the bad as well as the good and enjoy this journey that can make us and our children stronger than we ever dreamed.

PART 1

LOOK FOR LIGHT IN THE TRENCHES

. . . those seemingly endless trenches of motherhood

will be gone before you know it

TRENCHES DON'T LAST

Shawni

One of my favorite essays on motherhood is by Pulitzer Prize–winning author Anna Quindlen, who writes:

"Everything in all the books I once pored over is finished for me now. Penelope Leach. Berry Brazelton. Dr. Spock. The ones on sibling rivalry and sleeping through the night and early childhood education, all grown obsolete. Along with *Goodnight Moon* and *Where the Wild Things Are,* they are battered, spotted, well used. But I suspect that if you flipped the pages, dust would rise like memories."

Later, Quindlen writes about some of the mistakes she made while raising her babies: "The biggest mistake I made is the one that most of us make. . . . I did not live in the moment enough. This is particularly clear now that the moment is gone, captured only in photographs. There is one picture of the three of [my children] sitting in the grass on a quilt in the shadow of the swing set on a summer day, ages six, four, and one. And I wish I could remember what we ate, and what we talked about, and how they sounded, and how they looked when they slept that night. I wish I had not been in such a hurry to get on to the next thing: dinner, bath, book, bed. I wish I had treasured the doing a little more and the getting it done a little less" (*Loud and Clear,* 8, 10–11).

I remember the moment her words became some of my favorites. I was pregnant and had two young children only fourteen months apart. I was overwhelmed. I couldn't keep up. Without fail, our two babies seemed to need opposite things at exactly the same time. I found that as much as I was in love with these kids, I was chock full of the "I can't wait untils." I couldn't wait until Max could just feed himself or until Elle could sit up and entertain herself for a second. It seemed to me that it would be pure heaven when I could sleep through a night uninterrupted until 7:00 in the morning.

I had been skimming through my *Newsweek,* trying desperately to catch a glimpse into the real world—that world that had become foreign to me in many ways ever since I took on the title of *Mother.* Amongst the articles about politics and world affairs was Ms. Quindlen's article.

As soon as I read the above excerpt, tears came pouring down my cheeks. Yes, I'm sure some pregnancy hormones were involved in my outburst, but most of it was the pure realization that I wasn't living in the moment enough. Sure, the trenches of motherhood I was slogging through at that particular time in my life were deep. I couldn't see out. There was no light whatsoever at the end of the tunnel (at least not on that day). But when I came to that paragraph I was struck with the thought that I needed to find the light in my trench of motherhood. I needed to soak up my babies. Because if Anna Quindlen was wishing she'd cherished the moment a little more, I was sure I'd be right there with her if I didn't get my act together and enjoy the now a little more. Her trenches were gone . . . nothing but a faded memory. Mine were still deep, and I was going to live it up in there.

So I did an experiment with my two small children. One day I just slowed down. I changed gears. Instead of trying to fit in a million different errands and social things, I stayed home with my kids for a day. We read books, popped popcorn, sang songs, put together puzzles, and just delighted in being with each other. And I noticed so much more. Elle spilled her drink all over her beloved "blankie" and started to cry when I told her I had to wash it (taking away those blankies for long enough to wash them was always a trick). Max leaned over to her and told her in the sweetest voice that it was OK and that he would share his blankie with her while hers was in the washing machine. I noticed that Elle's sweet dimple when she smiled is about the cutest thing in the world. I complimented Max on so many things he did well that day and watched him beam. I was so in love with being a mom I could hardly contain myself.

Well, of course the next day was different. I had to catch up on things I had neglected the day before—much to my chagrin, life hadn't stopped while I was busy living in the moment! Max and Elle teased each other constantly, and Elle drew all over the couch with a ballpoint pen. But for some reason it didn't really bother me much. Sure, I was frustrated, but I realized that even the catastrophes are moments that will fade and will most likely bring on a melancholy smile in the future. My mind had made a shift. I still have to keep remembering to keep that shift in focus, but that's half the battle.

It's true that as a mother there is always a never-ending list of things to accomplish. Pay the bills. Check. Do the dishes. Check. Make dinner. Check. Do the shopping. Check. But are we successful if we didn't notice the look on our child's face when he learned to "pump" on the swing by himself? Is it success if we got lunch done and put the kids down for naps in fifteen minutes' time so we could finish catching up on "important projects" if we forgot to help the kids finish the puzzle we promised we would? Sometimes success is when we *don't* get through the to-do list but instead stop long enough to notice the little things. To savor moments. Not only to notice the delight in our children's eyes, but to help *create* that delight.

In her book *Surrendering to Motherhood,* author Iris Krasnow writes that the most important advice she could give mothers is to Be There. She says: "I know that I'm fortunate to be in a profession and marriage that allows me to spend most of each day near my children. But Being There isn't about money or even about staying home full-time. It's about an emotional and spiritual shift, of succumbing to Being Where You Are When You Are, and Being There as much as possible. It's about crouching on the floor and getting delirious over the praying mantis your son just caught instead of perusing a fax [or filling the dishwasher] while he is yelling for your attention and you distractedly say over your shoulder: 'Oh, honey, isn't that a pretty bug.'

"It's about being attuned enough to notice when your kid's eyes shine so you can make your eyes shine back" (170).

I want my kids to see my eyes shine when I play with them. I want to enjoy their play as much as they do. I want to "crouch down on the floor and get delirious" over the seemingly simple things that delight them. I want to look at the world through their eyes. I want to be *theirs* while I can.

I know that no matter how much I write about the funny things I want to remember, no matter how many pictures I take and stash in photo albums, no matter how much I will time to slow down and beg my kids to quit growing so darn fast, this time with young children will still slip away. But the *joy* that I *let* myself feel while I'm in the moment with my kids will not fade with the years like the pictures and the memories; it will become part of me. It will become part of my children.

Of course I must realize that no matter how many good intentions I have, I'll still have days of frustration where I'm too tired to pull out the paints *again* and let the kids mess up my freshly cleaned kitchen *again*. It will still be frustrating to find Tide laundry detergent spread all over the laundry room floor and filling up the bottom of the dryer. It will always take time to get everyone out the door with hair brushed and shoes on. But before I know it I won't have those things to make my life crazy anymore. And believe it or not, I'm gonna miss them! The secret is that savoring the crazy day-to-day moments, whether they be sentimental, sweet moments or moments of pure mayhem, makes motherhood rich and rewarding.

THE BIG PICTURE

Linda

There were a lot of years when I thought I would never walk by the diaper aisle at the grocery store without stocking up. I was sure that the days of not being able to find the binky and the never-ending frustrations of doing those important "Star of the Week" posters for a child who just remembered at 10 P.M. that he had to have it by the next morning would never end. I dreamed of the days that I would be able to sleep in instead of waking to an annoying alarm clock and dragging myself out of bed after only four or five hours of sleep because of a sick child or a fussy baby or finishing a project in those quiet hours after the house slept. Those mornings were full of urging kids over and over—and sometimes not too nicely—to get out of bed, to practice, to finish homework, to get themselves ready, to put their dishes in the dishwasher instead of on the counter.

I hated the inevitable panic every morning of somebody not being able to find shoes when they were already late for school and the inevitable wailing over lost homework and the sibling rivalry. I finally decided that I'd better get used to it because I could see no end! On the very hardest days, I promised myself that, if this ever did end, I would *never* forget how hard raising children really was!

Then, suddenly, but also gradually (those empty nest moms will know what I mean) all those days *did* come to an end. Diapers, science projects, posters, chaotic mornings, babies who wouldn't sleep through the night, little kids always in my face while I was on the phone, as well as teenagers with a crisis a minute and who came in late, came to a halt. Kids left one by one, came back one by one, and left again for good . . . so far.

I walked out of the trenches with a big smile, thinking everything from here on in would be a piece of cake. Though many things did get a lot easier—laundry, for example, and less daily stress—I quickly learned that parenting never really ends; it just gets different, and in many ways better. I am back in the swing of changing diapers—my grandchildren's—but I don't have to buy them!

Though none of our children ever became concert violinists, pianists, harpists, trumpeters, or drummers, they do all have an appreciation for music that I have convinced myself they would not have without all those crazy hours of forced practice and tears dripping down the piano keys. I now *love* watching my grandchildren practice and do their "Star of the Week" charts—at the last minute—and I giggle when I see them frantically looking for shoes on the way out the door to school. Déjà vu!

Even though I do occasionally get to sleep in and don't have to worry about lost homework and kids climbing out of the carts and knocking the displays down at the grocery store, life is still stressful. But it's a different kind of stress. There is always a child who is worried about one of their children, one who is having a hard time finding "the perfect partner" to marry, another who is worried about a horrendous situation with a lawsuit over which he has absolutely no control. Indeed, when the kids leave home, stress becomes different and things get bigger.

Let me explain what I mean by bigger. All of our children live far away from us, so we have loved being able to get them together during the month of July at a place that we love and where I happened to have been born and raised: Bear Lake, Idaho. We have six married children who live in hot, muggy places in the summer, so we are truly blessed to have the moms come to Bear Lake as long as possible during July (different years, different amounts of time). It is so fabulous to have a time to talk with grown daughters and incredible daughters-in-law and to watch the cousins interact, to observe sibling rivalry—and even cousin rivalry—without being in charge of the resolution and to watch with delight the comings and goings, strugglings, disciplinings, weepings, and wailings without feeling stressed about having to figure out how to solve the problems.

At some point in the month all the dads and singles join us for four days of wild fun and complete chaos! The details surrounding such a gathering are mind-boggling. Last summer from July 1 to August 1 we had between twenty and thirty-six people at our house at Bear Lake every day. During the four days of our reunion we had thirty-three men, women, and children for three meals a day (this included seventeen kids aged eleven and under). When the dads went back to work, aunts, uncles, cousins, and friends filed in. Because it was an hour round-trip drive to the nearest grocery store, we had brought food in by the truckload! In a ten-day period we figured that we served about 840 meals!

Of course it wasn't all about food. It was also about sand castles, horse rides, blowing bubbles, long talks on the beach, and watching the kids dig enough holes in the sand to reach China if they were all strung together.

In addition it was about throwing up and diarrhea. Every year we have some sort of "bug" going around. From one room would come a blood-curdling scream from an eighteen-month-old with a bottom that looked like raw meat after several days of "the runs." In the laundry room where one of the two-and-a-half-year-old twins slept, there was vomit, luckily over the edge of the pack-and-play and onto the slate floor.

Those incredible moms were up all night with children spewing out one end or the other and arose exhausted but loving those kids all the more. They cleaned up endless piles of Cheerios and spilled apple juice, accounted for up to five mouths to be fed before they put a bite into their own, and did so without a murmur. All day they helped resolve conflicts and prepared food when it was their turn. They bit their lips (only occasionally "freaking out") when dealing with a child at an annoyingly stormy stage! There *was* a certain amount of angst from the mother of the two-year-old twins when one little renegade escaped unnoticed and, reaching up as far as his tippy toes could take him, meticulously colored the outside of the new white family mini-van with an orange crayon. As promised, I had not really forgotten how hard motherhood was; but it takes being thrown back into the daily crisis routine to help me thoroughly remember.

Through all the craziness of our last summer trip, I stepped back and was absolutely amazed that after all those years of parenting, I was watching my own children be parents. What a delight—as well as a responsibility—it was to learn that almost nothing is more important than keeping your mouth shut when you would do things a different way!

After it was all over and I had looked through about two thousand digital pictures of our precious few days together (we have five quite amazing photographers), I chuckled at the sometimes smiling, sometimes howling children's faces and couldn't help but feel the joy of the moments captured in those pictures full of light and love (and just a little bit of diarrhea running down one little leg) and I thought of what an amazing journey motherhood is. Yes, some days "motherhood is like being pecked to death by a duck" (an anonymous quote my sister has hanging in her hall), but the secret is that eventually your efforts will start to count. Sooner than you can realize now, you'll be watching your children having children and will be amazed at how much better they are than you were and that somewhere, somehow, you must have done something good!

IMAGINATION

Shawni

Sometimes you've got to have a little imagination to get you through the trenches. You've also got to enjoy the imagination your kids are naturally full of. There's not a lot that will brighten a dreary morning like walking in on your three-year-old daughter after the breakfast chaos to find her in the midst of a serious acting out session. Her fork has become a beautiful princess and her last bite of pancakes is an evil monster. Melts my heart every time.

My dad has quite an imagination, and I'm so glad he's passed part of it on to me and my kids. Growing up we spent countless hot summer nights in our first rustic little cabin at gorgeous Bear Lake. My brothers and sisters and I would be lying on our nifty fold-out-from-the-wall-hand-crafted-by-our-dad beds on top of our foam mats. We would be hot—our faces beet red from a day at the beach with no sunscreen—and we'd be worn out from our "summer job" of carrying rocks up from the beach to line our makeshift front patio. We'd lay still, in hopes that the air from the big fan in the window would reach us and cool us down.

But it wasn't the heat we were thinking about. It was what sort of imaginative and crazy story our dad would come up with to tell us that night. He'd sit in the red chair in the corner and spill out the most glorious tales full of all kinds of adventure. There was this boy named after a combination of all my brother's names who would save the world all the time. There were the adventures of another family who looked just like us in "Mirror Land," always so creative and chock full of stuff to keep us hooked. Our dad would get to the most intense part of the story and then he'd say, "to be continued tomorrow." Oh, how I hated those stories to end!

Part of our wonder with them was that our dad is the greatest storyteller of all time. Part was the fact that we got to stay up a little longer to hear the adventures. But mostly I think we liked to hear the smooth, deep velvety sound of our dad's voice so close to us as we went to sleep.

Growing up we'd also have really interesting "characters" who would sometimes visit to tuck us into bed at night. They mysteriously reminded us of our dad, but they dressed in crazy outfits and their names were things like "Horsey Lorsey," "Monster Man," and "Serapoo." They lived at the North Pole with Santa Claus, but they'd kindly come visit us all year long and didn't limit their magic to the Christmas season.

Inspired by my imaginative dad, our family also has some friends in "Mirror Land."

In this land, there's this family called the Spunks. They are exactly like us: a mom, a dad, one boy, and four crazy girls. The weird thing is that not only is this family just like ours on paper, but they look exactly like us too. We can see the Spunks any time we want, just by looking in the mirror. It's amazing. And when we're peeking in on them, they copy everything we do. It's completely magic!

There are just a few small differences between our family and theirs. First, instead of their names being Max, Elle, Grace, Claire, and Lucy, they are called Hunk, Flower, Sparkle, Butterfly, and Chub-e-rooster (please note that I had no say over the names). Oh, and their dad's name is Grump-apotomus (self-named), and their mom's name is Pixie (her dad gave her that one when she was their age).

The other difference is that, in Mirror Land, the family just like ours works together perfectly. When their mom asks them to do their jobs, within minutes, Voila! They're done. They don't have any fighting, and they're always kind to each other.

I know it's almost impossible to comprehend, but our family here in the real world doesn't always work like that! The kids have been forgetting to make their beds in the morning. They've been throwing clothes on the floor when they change. They've been leaving scraps of drawings and crayons all over the place. So the other night after Grace and Claire had to miss out on story time before bed because their room was so messy that we had to spend our reading time picking things up instead of snuggling together with a book, I let them in on some very important details about their mirror twins, Sparkle and Butterfly. Because, as chance would have it, they had the same issue a while ago. But they learned their lesson and now their room is always clean. Those mirror girls realized that it was so much easier to just put their clothes away or in the hamper right when they took them off rather than letting things pile up, making a bigger mess to clean up. And now they're always happy because they get to play with friends after school and every night they get to have story time since they keep their room so darn spic and span.

And guess what? The magic transferred from Mirror Land into our land! The last few days Grace and Claire's room has been spotless when Grace leaves for school. And do you know what else? It's always spotless at night, too, so we can have a long story time just like Sparkle and Butterfly do.

We'll see how long this lasts, but for now, boy oh boy, I love those good examples in Mirror Land.

If we remember to let some imagination in every once in a while, motherhood is just more fun. Who knows, if we get really good at it, we may be able to even imagine that those dark trenches transform into walls of flowers!

WIT'S END

Shawni

If anyone wants to know what a place called Wit's End looks like, just ask me. I visit there quite often.

It's amazing how, in motherhood, you can go from feeling like you could conquer the world one day to wishing you could curl up in a corner and give up the next.

The fact that life never slows down doesn't help.

Most days I am in permanent *on* mode. It begins in the morning as I sit on the piano bench helping the older kids plunk out new pieces on the piano, then moves to the phone call with the doctor's office that forgot to fax a blood work order to the lab, then on to changing the sheets on Elle's bed for a visitor, to changing Claire's sheets because she wet the bed—again—to cajoling the kids to clean up after themselves while trying to positively reinforce how great it is to have a clean house, to dropping everything I'm trying to juggle every time one of Lucy's therapists comes over, to comforting a crying child, to editing a photo shoot, to figuring out the best way to deal with naughty behavior from a particular child, to trying to build up another child who seems to have low self-esteem—and that's all before dinnertime.

The list goes on and on and on. Most of it consists of good, fulfilling things. And when the tasks come at me a few at a time I can take them on, no problem. I can handle it. That's what moms do, right?

But there are some weeks when the "to dos" feel like they've been poured on by the bucketful and I just can't keep up. Fortunately, I can always count on the fact that tomorrow's going to be better. I just know it. Because it *almost* always is. Max will say something to make me laugh. Claire will give me a hug and tell me she loves me out of the blue. Dave will wink at me from across the room. And suddenly all the *on* time will seem worth it.

I love this quote from Victor Hugo:

"Have courage for the great sorrows of life and patience for the small ones; and when you have laboriously accomplished your daily task, go to sleep in peace. God is awake."

It makes me feel at peace knowing that after I've done the very best I can do, there's someone more powerful that can fill in the gaps.

I guess the secret is to realize that yes, we mothers visit a place called Wit's End quite regularly; but all the time we spend there makes the precious moments when we come "home" that much better.

THE REFINER'S FIRE

Linda

Reading Shawni's previous secret about the way to escape Wit's End reminds me of what an education we receive in the process of raising our children! When asked how I survived all those years and all those children, I usually answer, "One day at a time!" The astounding thing to me and the great secret of our mothering experience is that through the hard times, *we* are the ones who benefit most!

I always smile when I think of the following little story written by a young mother: "It was one of the worst days of my life. The washing machine broke down, the telephone kept ringing, my head ached, and the mail carrier brought a bill I had no money to pay. Almost to the breaking point, I lifted my one-year-old into his high chair, leaned my head against the tray, and began to cry. Without a word, my son took his pacifier out of his mouth and stuck it in mine" (Clara Null, in *Chicken Soup for the Working Woman's Soul,* 231).

After a particularly grueling day of her own, one of our daughters e-mailed me the gory details. She claimed that most of the time since the baby was born she had felt totally overwhelmed, inadequate, ineffective, unorganized, frazzled, and helpless. I e-mailed her back and reminded her about the most amazing side-effect of motherhood: the Refiner's fire!

A beautiful piece of fine pottery could be easily chipped and broken were it not for the blazing fire of the kiln that toughens and strengthens and refines it. And though mothers the world over feel chipped and broken on a daily basis, it is their very trials and difficulties that toughen, strengthen,

and refine them. Learning to accept the hardships in our paths as stepping-stones and ways to improve our skills is a great secret to our success! That fire makes us more patient, less judgmental, more tolerant, less critical, more able to multitask, less worried about details, less structured, more serendipitous, more organized, and—when needed—OK with being less organized.

Over time, the grueling job of a mother requires one to learn everything from patience to clinical psychology. It teaches you to roll with the punches, pick your battles, and fish a favorite toy out of a toilet that has been used but not flushed without a wince. You become a non-judgmental driver, a nurse, and a comforter. And, with a little self-reminder, you can recognize "a stage" and leap over the exceedingly strange behavior of a child with a single bound.

When you are "in the fire," it is sometimes hard to recognize the value of what you are learning. But the day-by-day refining process, the problem solving, crisis resolution, mental stretching, mess clean-ups, sleep deprivation, and loving more than you ever thought possible truly makes you into a smart, aware, beautifully refined individual.

The great secret is appreciating the refined person you are becoming through your trials. I love the thought that what won't kill you will make you better! So perhaps if we know that secret and even welcome the hard times, life won't seem nearly as difficult.

As Elder Orson F. Whitney taught: "No pain that we suffer, no trial that we experience is wasted. It ministers to our education, to the development of such qualities as patience, faith, fortitude and humility. All that we suffer and all that we endure, especially when we endure it patiently, builds up our character, purifies our hearts, expands our souls, and makes us more tender and charitable, more worthy to be called the children of God. . . . And it is through sorrow and suffering, toil and tribulation that we gain the education that we come here to acquire" (as quoted in Kimball, *Faith Precedes the Miracle*, 98).

So forge on, Moms . . . and remember that as you experience the everyday trials of motherhood, "the fire" you are navigating will make *you* shine!

MOMENTS

Shawni

Little things make me smile. And sometimes (well, most of the time) I forget to write them down. Little things, like how Lucy straightens her legs and points her toes (pressing her chunky thighs together) when I lay her down to change her diaper, or how Grace has to do a little dance in front of the mirror (while singing some silly song to herself) in her towel after every bath so she can gear up to get her pajamas on. I want to remember this stuff. I want to cherish these moments while they last. These moments are the light that gets me through the trenches some days.

There is strength to be gained in soaking in the little moments. Strength comes from dropping everything and reading with your nine-year-old because you realize she's more important than any other project you may be working on. From watching two of your children who are usually at each other's throats on a day when they're getting along. From watching the glow on your child's face when his dad praises him for mowing the lawn well. From letting yourself get caught up in the music your toddlers are dancing to in pure delight. That strength—and how to build it—is all part of the secret of enjoying and loving life as a mother of small children, a lassoer of chaos.

There was a day shortly following Christmas one year that I remember well. I finally got myself and my two at-home-during-the-day kids to the mall for some post-Christmas returns and exchanges. It wasn't fun. The baby was doing all kinds of acrobatics in the stroller, and poor

Claire had hurt her knee on the trampoline the day before and kept whining that she couldn't walk. So as I carried her through the mall in one arm while trying to contort my other arm enough to successfully maneuver my stroller laden with bags and a chunky baby, I noticed a mother with a new little baby, maybe a month old. He was fussy and she was trying to comfort him while maneuvering her stroller too. Oh, I wanted to just ask her if I could hold him and snuggle him for a little bit. I wished I had my old Baby Bjorn to hand over to her. I could never go to the mall without it when I had babies that little. And then the thought of having my tiny snuggling babies right next to me while I did my daily tasks started eating at me. How they looked when they were sleeping, how they smelled, how they sighed in their sleep, and yes, even their sweet little newborn cries. Baby hunger crept in. "How could those days have passed so quickly?" I asked myself in awe as I looked at my own crying "baby" and her whimpering sister sidekick.

And then a thought struck me. A few years from now I'll be roaming the mall, and all my kids will be in school. Yes, it will be nice. It'll seem so free and strange in a good way. But, at that moment in the mall I realized that on that day in the future when I'm wandering the mall all fancy-free, there's no doubt I'll run into my double self from that post-Christmas shopping day. She'll be wrestling with her toddlers with a frustrated look on her face, assuring them that they're almost done with the errands of the day. And oh, will I ever wish I could go back, at least for a little while, and slow life down while I snuggle those kids up and kiss their chubby cheeks. I'll try to envision them as their little selves climbing on me all whiney and needy, and I'll probably tear up a little just like I am right now because I'll miss those little people. I know the bigger form of my little people will be wonderful. I can't wait to "meet" them and grow with them. But for now, how grateful I am that I can recognize how much I need to cherish each moment—snotty noses, messy faces, dramatics, and all that craziness in one great big package with a bow. Because when I blink they'll be all grown up. But those moments that I cherished will still be there.

something that one of your kids said or did. It might be taking a minute to enjoy a gorgeous sunset. It might be getting a call from a long lost friend, just when you thought it was so important to accomplish something else. An annoying interruption by a child becomes an opportunity!

My Richard has written a whole book on this topic called *Spiritual Serendipity,* which, simply put, says that the best things in life usually aren't planned. Every challenge has a "serendipity." If you have a flat tire on the freeway with the soccer team in tow and a kind person stops to help, thus inspiring you to return the favor some day, that's a serendipity. If you are watching for serendipities, they happen every day, *and* they make life so much more fun! When you get really good at looking for serendipity, instead of rolling over in the morning with your first thought being a heavy, "What do I have to do today?" you might be able to roll over and think, "I wonder what's going to happen to me today?" That makes life more of an adventure than drudgery.

It takes time to develop these habits, but it's worth the persistence! Good luck with your short list of three and finding serendipity in your life. Though you'll still have to spin those plates, you'll find that you feel more balanced and that you're having a lot more fun than you thought you were!

ENOUGH IS ENOUGH

Shawni

Each year as the school year winds down I make the same goal: to let my kids be kids for the summer, to let them have time for their imaginations to run wild and have downtime. I have big plans to hang out, just the six of us, and go to the library and have our own kind of field trips. Each year I make a commitment that I'm not going to over-schedule the summer like I did the year before. Yep, every year that's my goal. And without fail, every year I end up being frustrated. Because all of a sudden, once again, these kids are mysteriously signed up for everything under the sun.

It's not only summer that offers tantalizing classes like swim team and various sports camps. During the school year there's gymnastics, piano, tennis, cooking classes, acting classes, art classes, and singing classes. You name it, there's a class for it, and man, oh, man those classes are pretty darn tempting!

And it's not even just the kids who are begging for them a lot of the time! It's me thinking, "Oh, this would be so great for so-and-so." I struggle because all those things really could help my kids learn a lot. Who knows, maybe Elle will be an awesome volleyball player if I just sign her up for volleyball camp. She's going to be so tall, maybe that's her "calling," and she would miss out on it if I didn't let her go. Maybe we'll uncover that Grace is a natural actress (put in practice by all her daily dramatics) if she takes that acting class. And Max, he's quite an artist, wouldn't that art class give him some great confidence? And poor Claire, my fourth child who doesn't get to do many lessons—I keep having this feeling that if we put her in a gymnastics class she really could take off . . . she seems to have inherited a little more of Dave's coordination than mine, which could really help her in the long run!

The list goes on and on. How do you find the balance between what to put your kids in— and thus experience the world and magnify their talents—and keeping them at your side, cherishing that time as long as you can and letting them just be kids?

I think the real secret is to just slow down. Enough is really enough. Sometimes what kids really need most is unstructured time and space. My rule of thumb (when I'm not letting myself get carried away by all those inviting lessons) is that each child can have one music-based lesson and one physical lesson (sports, gymnastic, etc.). And sometimes I wonder why I even do that much. It's great to expose our kids to all that we can. But really, there's not much more that can give our kids confidence and encouragement than spending time with a mother who loves them.

PRAYER WORKS

Linda and Shawni

Linda: Last year Richard and I had the opportunity to speak in Istanbul. Our little hotel there was literally across the street from the famous Blue Mosque, named for the hundreds of thousands of blue tile mosaics housed in this breathtakingly enormous edifice. Each morning we were awakened at exactly sunrise (about 6:15 AM) by a dedicated Muslim leader of the faith pronouncing the three-minute "Call to Prayer" over an enormous loud speaker. I was amazed and inspired by the dedication it takes for a loyal Muslim to consistently heed that call to prayer five times a day. Our seminar participants in Muslim countries left workshops to retire to their rooms where they addressed Allah, facing east on prayer rugs, and then returned to the seminar and continued taking notes. Oh, that we were all that dedicated to prayer!

Our youngest daughter, who is a missionary in England, is an inspiration to us in dedication to faith and prayer. She was asked by a family she was teaching if she thought her family would be about the same whether or not they believed in prayer and the principles taught by Jesus Christ. She answered with a resounding, "Absolutely not!" Our faith and prayers are our anchor as individuals as well as a family.

All of our nine children have had the rare opportunity of serving as missionaries all over the world. Counting the in-laws who have come into our family, many of whom have also served missions, "we" can speak eleven languages, and we find that our faith gives us joy beyond our ability to describe. The secret anchor of all that language learning, finding people who are receptive, teaching the principles of the gospel of Jesus Christ, and loving those both in and outside our faith was prayer.

In addition, our son Jonah has been the object of our prayers more than any other soul in our family. Let me name just a few challenging incidents in his life: he was born nine weeks early, attacked by two pit bulls at age eleven, and hit head-on by a car as he ran across the street at age sixteen. He continues to keep our prayers active and in progress!

When our kids were little we tried to have a little devotional every morning to read scriptures together for ten minutes before we started the minutia of breakfast and practicing. Some had gone back to sleep on a chair by the time we called for prayer. But something about the routine of knowing that we were praying together every day gave our kids a security that we have only lately come to appreciate.

I heard a speech once by Mrs. Norman Vincent Peale about their family synchronizing their watches at morning prayer so that they could pray for family members who had specific worries at certain times of the day. So we followed suit, and some mornings we would all agree to pray for Noah to do well on his math test at 9:20 or for Dad to do well in an important meeting at 1:30. It was a fun way to think and pray for each other during the day.

Initially, all those morning prayers were on our knees around the coffee table or the kitchen table, but as life got more hectic and basketball boys were leaving in the dark of the morning and getting home in the dark of the evening, we decided that whoever was leaving on those hectic school mornings should yell "huddle" as they were standing at the door. Whoever was in earshot met at the front door and, with arms around shoulders, we offered a quick prayer of thanksgiving and protection. Sometimes it was just one child and one parent, sometimes two or three or more joined the circle.

Today we have a group e-mail account where every family member is reached almost instantly at the touch of a button. There are often requests for prayers from one of our children in distress. We assure each other often that we are praying and sometimes fasting for them. Like those cyberspace messages that can't be seen as they fly through space, prayers reach their destination but with even better accuracy. True, prayers are not always answered as we would wish or as soon as we would like, but we believe that they are heard and answered in the Lord's way and time.

Shawni: As a mother, there are times I find myself pleading with Heavenly Father throughout the day: "*Please* help me be more patient," or "*Please* bless my kids who forgot their bike helmets to get to school safely," or "*Please, please, please* help me find my toddler in this crowded public place." I never really understood the admonition to pray all day, in public and in private, until I became a mother: until I held my first newborn in my arms night after night, pleading with Heavenly Father to help him sleep so I could sleep, too. I always knew prayer worked, but I never felt that I needed it as much as I did once I hit the trenches of motherhood. I know that prayer works, because I've become infinitely more in tune to it since I need so much help daily. It's the most comforting thing in the world to know that someone is up there looking out for you. The secret is realizing that, and letting Him in.

As a young mother, I was inspired by Chieko N. Okazaki (one of my heroes). There is one specific address she gave called "Lighten Up!" that really changed me. She talked about how as mothers we tend to compartmentalize our lives. We have different cubbyholes for different things: family, church, gardening, and so on. She said instead of thinking of our spiritual lives as one of our cubbies, it should be more like the scent in the air that drifts through all the rooms. She relates this story:

"Suppose the Savior comes to visit you. You've rushed around and vacuumed the guest room, put the best sheets on the bed, even got some tulips in a vase on the dresser. Jesus looks around the room, then says, 'Oh, thank you for inviting me into your home. Please tell me about your life.'

"You say, 'I will in just a minute, but something's boiling over on the stove, and I need to let the cat out.'

"Jesus says, 'I know a lot about cats and stoves. I'll come with you.'

"'Oh, no,' you say. 'I couldn't let you do that.' And you rush out, carefully closing the door behind you.

"And while you're turning down the stove, the phone rings, and then Jason comes in with a scrape on his elbow, and the visiting teacher supervisor calls for your report, and then it's suppertime, and you couldn't possibly have Jesus see that you don't even have placemats, for Pete's sake, and someone forgot to turn on the dishwasher so that you're eating off paper plates, and then you have to drive Lynne to her basketball game. So by the time you get back to the room where Jesus is still patiently waiting for you, you're so tired that you can barely keep your eyes open—let alone sit worshipfully at Jesus' feet to wait for those words of profound wisdom and spiritual power to wash over you, to make you different, to make everything else different—and you fall asleep whispering, 'I'm sorry. I'll try to do better. I'm so sorry'" (in *Women and Christ: Living the Abundant Life*, 6).

Isn't this how we are as mothers? When we really need the Savior's guidance the most, sometimes we tend to shut it out. The secret is to use prayer to our advantage. Let the Savior "follow" us around and help us out when we're at the end of our ropes. That is when prayer really works!

PART 2

HAVE AN ORGANIZED OFFENSE

. . . before serious defense becomes necessary

A PLAN FOR YOU

Linda

When I got married thirty-nine years ago I was clueless about how important an organized offense would be in successful mothering. It took a while for me to realize that part of that offense had to do with making a plan to help me progress as a person.

As young mothers, even though we can somehow make time for our kids' playgroups, music lessons, and sports activities; our husband's errands; grocery shopping; Cub Scouts; our church and community responsibilities; keeping the house in some semblance of order; and a thousand other daily responsibilities, often the hardest thing to find time for is ourselves! Sometimes I feel like a gerbil on a wheel, running as fast as my feet will carry me hour after hour and, at the end of the day, ending up just where I started! Mothers often feel exhausted, powerless to change anything, and without a plan to make things any better. The important thing for mothers in this situation is to remember something a friend taught me in a mothering seminar: You are the greatest asset your family has. In taking care of yourself, you preserve that asset. That is a business term, but it applies perfectly to our role as mothers.

Three secrets have saved my sanity when it has come to taking care of me through the years. Though I wasn't always perfect in the execution of the plan, here they are:

The first is that from the time Richard and I were married, every Sunday we had what we called a "Sunday Session." This consisted of his keeping the kids from pounding down the door for half an hour while I locked myself in my room to contemplate my plans for the coming week (and then I did the same for him). I categorized my goals in three sections (this has already been explained in more detail in the Balancing Act secret). I first wrote a short list of the things needed to do for myself. Second, I wrote some things that I needed to do for my family, and third I wrote down what I need to accomplish for my work/service for the week. Then I would try to plug in a plan for accomplishing those goals each day. What day should I do the Mommy Date? When could I take flowers to a neighbor with a new baby? When could I spend some uninterrupted time with my husband?

Even though I didn't always check my goals every day, just having them in my mind helped me to stay on track. I'm sure I succeeded more often than I would have had I not given it some thought and written down specific goals.

The second thing that helped me most as a young mother was to have what I would call "A Day Away." Once a year and, later, sometimes even twice a year, Richard would help me arrange to get away for a day or a part of a day to do some "life planning." Usually I would actually go to a motel or hotel room, depending on our budget for the year. Sometimes I would just take my planning journal and sit in the van in a lovely park for the afternoon. There I had some great quality time to assess where I was and where I was going . . . as a mother and as a person.

I did an inventory of the five facets of my life (see the Five-Facet Review secret for details). I thought about how I was doing physically, mentally, emotionally, socially, and spiritually. I thought about each of the kids and their needs and what I wanted to do to make our time together as much quality as it was quantity. I read. I caught up on the news. I wrote. Sometimes I even took a nap! It was a time of rejuvenation and determination to do better and even to figure out that I was doing pretty well in some areas. It was usually on a Saturday so Richard could stay with the kids. And when I got home, I was a new woman—refreshed and recharged. He was much more handsome than I had remembered when I left the chaos in his hands. Not only that, but he appreciated me more than I could have imagined. In addition, the kids were cuter, nicer, and even more manageable for several hours!

[Note from Shawni: My Dad was just absolutely a gem to let my mom get away like this. Although my husband is very supportive and wonderful, I have not been able to make this idea happen much at our house! But even though I can't get "A Day Away" like my mom did, I do really try to prioritize carving out time for my own "Sunday Session" once a week. It makes all the difference in my attitude and mindset to have planned out the future and to have a chance to think about my goals.]

Third, I always had a group of mothers that I met with regularly who were in a similar situation with their desires to be good mothers. They were stimulating and interesting and always inspired me to do better. As a young mother living in England, I vowed to gather mothers who wanted to be the best that they could be for occasional seminars. We had a chance to do that several times through our Homebase business in the years to come. We called them Home-Career Seminars.

In my wildest dreams, I could never have imagined at the time that our oldest daughter, Saren, would some day be doing something similar—only so much better! She and some friends have put together some great resources for mothers. Their Web site, The Power of Moms, provides a chance for moms to learn and share and offers materials to help you put together a really effective and fun "Learning Circle" of mothers that meets monthly. The Power of Moms also offers materials for putting together a "CareerMothers Seminar," where small groups of women who view motherhood as their primary career step away from their regular lives for a weekend to "recharge" as they share ideas and gain new perspectives. There's nothing like having meaningful discussions with other mothers dealing with the same "trenches" and joys of motherhood to buoy you up as a mother! For further information on how to set up a great mothers' group or hold your own CareerMothers Seminar, see the postscript at the end of this book.

So the secret is . . . take time for yourself and get away from it all once in a while. And spend time learning from and laughing with other mothers. You'll be a better mother because of it!

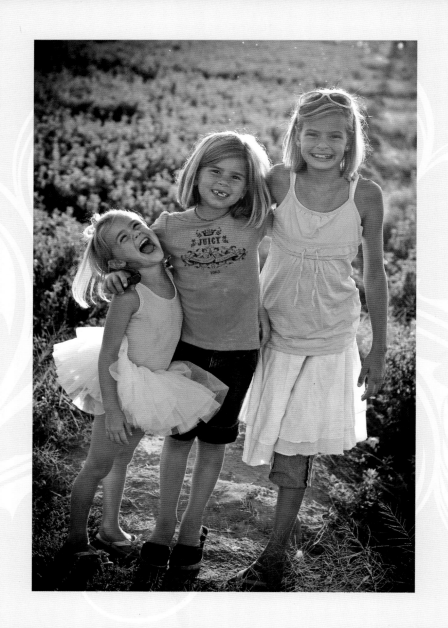

MISSION STATEMENTS

Linda

About fifteen years ago, with inspiration from our friends Stephen and Sandra Covey, we decided to make a concentrated effort to get our family together and hammer out a mission statement that everyone agreed on and helped to create. As the years have passed, we have realized that our efforts have helped our children have a sense of identity as a family. Having a family mission statement helped them to know that they were part of something bigger than themselves—a real, living, working family organization. It helped them know what we were about as a family . . . and where we were going!

We smile when we think about our first effort, which included renting a facility for two days and a night where we could have our whole family together to talk about creating a family mission statement. In our first formal meeting we asked the kids for their favorite words and ideas that we could use to create the things we wanted to accomplish as a family. Then we sent them off for an hour or two to swim, play ping-pong, or just relax and think about it. When we reconvened we exchanged ideas and started to craft what we thought we wanted for our family. At the end of the weekend, we had created a one-page mission statement that included everyone's ideas.

One problem: six months later when we met again at home to revisit the mission statement, nobody could remember just exactly what it said other than the words they had thought of themselves. So . . . we met again, this time just at home in a family meeting. We narrowed it down to just one paragraph. Six months later: still no one could remember many details of our paragraph. We realized we needed to simplify!

We remembered that one thing we had done during our initial meeting was to send each child off to his or her own corner to figure out his or her *own* personal mission statement. Those personal mission statements were terrific, and those were the ones they could remember! By then our son Talmadge was a teenager. This was his mission statement: "Return to God by living a life of service and example that incorporates a versatile, laid-back attitude that warms rather than intimidates others. Lead a family of reliable, pleasing, sensitive people who you can count on!" Though Tal has yet to find his eternal partner, he now perfectly personifies "the mission" he envisioned fourteen years ago.

The thing that we learned from having our kids create their own mission statements was that brevity was the key. In fact, we decided that we needed a family mission statement that was almost a mantra—an iron-clad few words that even a two-year-old could remember. What we came up with was three words long: "Broaden and contribute." Of course, the preliminaries helped to make those three words work. They were a combination of what we had all decided we wanted for our family.

Those three words have gone farther than we could ever have imagined! It meant that our children had committed to "broaden" themselves—to be dedicated to getting the best education they could, learn as much about other people and the world as possible, and discover different ways of thinking and ideas that were stimulating. It also meant they knew that it was our responsibility to give back, to go forward to contribute to the world in small and large ways. I won't enumerate all the details, but these words have paved the way for numberless ways to broaden and contribute.

We have challenged many parents to form a short, concise family mission statement that fits the ages of their children. A family in Canada saw us six months after our challenge and told us how much fun they were having with theirs—straight from the hearts of a six-year-old and a four-year-old: "Be thinkful, be thankful, and be bananas!" Perfect!

DINNERTIME

Shawni

Understanding the importance of dinnertime is a serious motherhood secret. Life is crazy, especially as kids grow older, and forcing a moment to sit down together can be pretty tough. We all know there are so many things that conflict with dinnertime togetherness. Sports and lessons and Scouts and friends and activities pull us in every different direction. Some nights we just can't squeeze it in no matter what we juggle around. But in our family we try our very best to make family dinnertime a priority. And that makes a big difference.

Growing up, my parents were a little wacky about dinnertime, and I loved it. My dad would have us stand up and give one-minute "speeches" on random subjects as part of our dinnertime activities. He'd have little games for us to play together. He'd have organized, thought-through topics he'd want to discuss. Dinnertime got pretty long some nights! I certainly can't live up to that in our family, especially since our kids are still pretty young, but one thing we have carried on is the idea of going around and telling each other our "Happies" and "Sads." Each night at dinner the kids tell us what their happiest and saddest or toughest moments were from the day. Claire is always the first to pipe right in; she *loves* it. Her happies and sads are inevitably that she was happy a friend could come over and she was sad when that same friend had to leave. But most of the time this ritual leads to good discussions and helps the kids tell us what really happened during the day instead of just saying it was "fine" or "good" or "bad." I like to hear the details, and this is a good way to squeeze them out.

Making dinnertime together a priority has a domino effect in our family. Not only do we spend more time together talking, we teach our kids more about manners (sometimes at dinnertime we turn our kitchen into a place we call the "Polite Café" (a great idea I got from a wise friend), which delights the kids and encourages them to have better manners), the importance of eating balanced meals, and the good habit of slowing down and enjoying our food rather than scarfing it down on our way to somewhere else. Because we make dinnertime together a priority, I make cooking a priority, too, and we eat more healthily because of it. This means I have to really try to put together ideas for meals in advance. The goal is to plan out meals for the week on Sunday night, but I must admit it doesn't always happen. It always works out best when I have something prepared early in the day that can just be put in the oven later; but sometimes (OK, most of the time) I'm scrambling at the last minute, and that's still OK. Sometimes, on really crazy days, I'll call my husband and have him pick something up on his way home from work. Even if we're eating take-out, we still sit at the table together and talk about our day. Because I cook a lot, I've started to spend a lot of time teaching my kids about cooking and getting them involved in the whole dinnertime process. My oldest two have started being in charge of cooking the meals once in a while, and they love it. They can make a mean chicken pot pie!

Some of my very best memories with my kids are sitting around the dinner table. When they were really little it was really nothing more than a few minutes of complete chaos, trying to get kids to stay sitting down, trying to put up nicely with the complaints about how they hate this particular dinner I'd spent a long time making and keeping them from smearing mashed potatoes all over their chairs. But I'm so glad we've made it a priority. It's become automatic, and because of that, it works. We talk about life. We laugh about things that happen. We bolster each other up. Last year I hung a huge world map on the wall right by our dining table. We talk about what's going on in the world. We talk about current events. Many of these discussions would not happen if we didn't make a point of having that time together.

If you're not a natural family dinner person, don't get overwhelmed! Start with one or two meals together a week and work from there. At our house, Friday night is pizza night. We always order or make pizza (it's part of family movie night). That helps us simplify.

The bottom line is that time together makes families stronger. And the secret is that family dinner is a great way to make time for each other.

MEETINGS

Linda and Shawni

How many of you have a meeting every week with your employees at work?" we always ask as we begin our seminars. Hands go up for almost every business owner and executive present. Next we ask, "How many of you have a meeting with your family every week?" It is amazing how seldom we see a raised hand!

Family meetings are the fertile soil where all the things included in this section can be "set up." When you think about it, it's hard to have a real, viable organization without a meeting. If you have just pre-schoolers, a ten-minute meeting is just perfect. Be sure to include refreshments! For older kids, half an hour is good. We always had an opening prayer and song, a planning session, and then someone gave a short lesson. You may want to spend several weeks setting up family laws (see the secret on Family Laws), introducing "Gunny Bag" (see the secret on Order), or doing a demonstration for a repenting bench (see the secret on Arguments). You may want to introduce a value you want to work on as a family that month or something you have learned spiritually that can be taught with simple visual aids.

Many of you will already be having terrific family meetings, but we all need a boost once in a while. Be prepared for a little chaos! It takes time and patience for the kids to get used to the idea of a formal meeting, but it's worth persistence!

There are so many resources for family meetings. If you run out of ideas, go to familynight lessons.com which is a Web site Richard and I have set up that provides five-minute lessons on joy and other values that your children can actually download and present themselves. Remember that ownership is the secret to a successful family meeting. Have your children conduct, give a lesson if possible, and prepare the treats (which are a very important part of the family meeting!).

Shawni and Dave are two of the best parents I know in having successful family meetings, so I'll have her finish this fun little secret to a successful family through having an organized offense.

Shawni: We have a family meeting every Sunday. Each child takes a turn conducting the meeting on a rotating basis. When our kids were really little, this was their very favorite part. We had a little stool they could stand up on and be "the boss." The conductor chooses someone to pick an opening song and someone else to say a prayer. Next, Dad is usually in charge of "Family Business," where everyone has a minute to tell the family what they're doing that week. I love this part because the kids really feel like they're important as they share things that are coming up that are important to them—even if it's something as seemingly insignificant as a class party they're having at school that week. Next is the "lesson," which is usually given by myself or my husband and is centered on something we've noticed needs to be discussed. Our kids are getting to the ages where they want to give the lessons, and we love it when they do.

The point is that we get to be together as a family. It creates a great forum for random as well as important things to be talked about. It's an offense that makes my kids feel like important parts of our family "whole," and we love it.

TRADITIONS

Shawni

Family traditions tie love strings around your family. And if you can start them early, they're one of the best-organized offenses you can come by.

We had some crazy traditions while I was growing up. One of my personal favorites was my dad's birthday tradition. His birthday fell in October, and he was the type who was enamored by fall leaves. I know, everyone loves the colors of fall. But my dad, serious nature lover, may win a prize on the depth of his love for his birthday season. So on his birthday we would rake up piles of leaves and jump in them. Simple, right? But we loved it. Whether it was in our own backyard, or at a park, or on a trip to a new place, we'd gather those leaves, throw them in the air, bury each other in them, and be together. Years passed, and some of us grew up and moved away. There was one particular year when my brother and sister and I were all in different countries on missions in England, Romania, and Bulgaria on my dad's birthday. I think it was the first year we missed being with the family on our big leaf-jumping day. With no coordination, we all sent my Dad a few of our favorite fall leaves in the birthday cards we mailed. And, boy howdy, does he ever still talk about that. The point is that not only did we miss him, we missed our tradition . . . that time with our family. And we wanted him to know that even though we were gone, our family was still together.

Another of my favorite traditions is my sister's annual "cake float." We usually ended up at Bear Lake around her birthday, so we had a birthday tradition of always floating her cake on the lake. She would take it out in the water, candles lit, on some floating thing we concocted, and then swim around with it. Somehow, the cake always made it out dry and delicious. She's continued that tradition every year, even when not at Bear Lake. I know, it's kind of wacky, but it's been one of the really lasting, fun traditions in our family. So when my daughter Elle was born on my sister's birthday, we jumped in on the tradition. It happens whether we're at Bear Lake or not (last year we had to do it in a swimming pool), and I love it because not only does it bind our family together, but it binds my kids with my family. Traditions are the best.

They don't need to be anything fancy. One Tuesday night last year I let my older kids stay up with me to swim laps in the pool. It turned out to be a magical night of togetherness, so we decided to form the "Tuesday Night Swim Club." My kids got to the point that they would look forward to it all week. They'd count down the days. It was such a great way to be "with" them. When it got too cold to continue, we had to give it up, but the second it started to warm up again they were on me to head out to the pool on Tuesday nights. They love it, and so do I.

We all have favorite Christmas traditions. I love that despite the busy-ness of the season, we are still able to fit in the true spirit of the season here and there, mostly due to the traditions that draw us to do things amidst the chaos. Christmas just wouldn't be the same without traditions, and my kids are old enough to push to make sure we do them. It's interesting to me to watch as they grow up how each year they latch firmer and tighter onto the few traditions we have so far and treasure them up, holding them so high. One of our favorite traditions is reading a Christmas story under the Christmas tree each night in December (well, the nights when we're home). A couple years ago Dave's brother's family gave us an awesome gift basket stuffed full of beautiful Christmas books, which has really added to our tradition. My kids think I'm nuts every once in a while when I can barely get through the ending of a book without tears streaming down my cheeks. There's nothing like nestling in there under the tree—so close that we're all touching—to read together.

So the secret is: family traditions are the glue that holds your family together—an offense that is much bigger than you can know until you look back and see the difference it has made.

FIVE-FACET REVIEW

Linda

More than three decades later, I still remember the overwhelming feelings that swept across me as I held our first little baby in my arms and thought about raising my child safely in this very scary world. How could I keep her safe from physical and emotional harm? What could I possibly do to ensure that she had a happy childhood and a socially secure and spiritually stable adolescence? I'd heard so many strong, committed parents of older children express their helpless feelings of horror as their children became involved in drugs, alcohol, and early sexual experimentation long before they were aware of it. I worried about how I could possibly be constantly aware of the needs of this little child in a world that was full of cunning and crafty influences that devalued the principles I felt were most important and trampled on the ideals that I held dear. I needed an offense!

Of course, there is absolutely no guarantee for keeping a child safe from the world. But I also know that one thing we did helped us to stay on top of what was going on in the lives of our children more than anything else. This was an idea that someone else suggested and for which I am so grateful. It started with a commitment Richard and I made to go on a date for dinner the first Friday of each month and have only one thing on our agenda: the kids. We called it "The Five-Facet Review." We would head for a restaurant with a little notebook in hand and, as soon as we were seated, start our review of the current status of each child. We went through five facets of their lives as we discussed how was each doing physically, mentally, socially, emotionally, and spiritually.

For example, we might say to each other, "How is Saydi doing physically?" Often we would agree that she was fine. But one month we realized that she may not be doing as well as she could in school. In our discussion we remembered that she had mentioned in passing that she could not see the blackboard very well. So thanks to our discussion, we got her to the optometrist, and her grades started to bounce back with the help of new glasses.

Sometimes we would get through all five facets of one child and really believe that he or she was doing well in all areas. But with another child, we would realize that there was a deep-seated shyness that needed our creative attention. Or we might discover that another was caving in to peer pressure and misbehaving in some way, so we needed to figure out a plan to help.

Now, you may say that with nine children and five facets to discuss about each one, we must have had to go to a Chinese restaurant with fifteen courses to get through it all. Not really. When the meal was finished we had only three or four things written in our notebook that each of us had agreed to work on with different children.

The experience was good for both of us. I learned things that I didn't realize I knew as Richard questioned me and we reasoned together about what to do to work out a current problem. Richard learned a lot about what was going on while he was at work and not down in the day-to-day trenches. It was a great time for him to be the problem solver and for us to exchange ideas and to really think about each child in detail. I must admit that we sometimes did our reviews in the car on trips rather than during dinners, and there were months that we missed. But having that time to work as partners to fill the needs of our children lent a special bond to our relationship, and it helped us see the individual needs and strengths of our children. Not only did we realize problems we could solve, we talked about things our kids were doing well and we were able to compliment them and build them up in those areas.

Some husbands are already involved in the intimate details of child rearing, which will make it all the more fun. But the concern we hear most often from moms is the need to get their husbands more involved in "raising the kids." Most husbands are natural problem solvers but are sometimes just waiting to be asked for advice and help. [Note from Shawni: I love having five-facet reviews, but I kind of have to sneak them in on my husband. He doesn't like doing something big and formal like my parents did, but he perks right up when I bring up the five facets in a really casual way. And he seems to notice things that have never occurred to me. I love seeing things from his perspective. Do whatever works for your relationship and your situation.]

Whatever your circumstances, if you haven't tried it before, the challenge is to have a five-facet review for your child or children, whether you have one or nine, whether your child is one or eighteen, whether you are married or single. If you are a single parent, do the review with a grandparent or friend who loves your child or children. If you have an ex-husband who's still involved with the kids, suggest that you might do a five-facet review occasionally so that you can feel you are on the same page when dealing with your children separately.

Even though Richard and I weren't able to catch every problem, it was a great way to catch a lot of problems that could have easily gotten out of control. In hindsight, I think that this monthly ritual has been an enormous safety net for our children—a great offense to catch little problems before they became big and substantially lessened the amount of defense needed down the road.

CREATING GREAT MEMORIES

Shawni

Sometimes, as part of an organized offense, you just have to create a good memory. Great memories hold families together, and when you first introduce a plan of action to create them (if your kids are like mine), you may be met with some resistance.

My parents knew this secret from the start. They did things with us that sometimes made us kick and scream. We whined. We complained. We begged them to leave us alone and let us have "normal" lives.

Luckily, they didn't listen.

They packed all nine of us up and took us to camp out in the mountains one summer while we built a log cabin. I was a teenager. There were tons of bugs. There was no shower.

My parents' writing career meant that we had the rare opportunity to travel around the world. They took us to live in England for six months right after I had gotten my extremely shy self settled into high school. I cried every day for the first month. I wrote desperate letters to my friends. I bawled when we had to go shopping for the dark-brown school uniform I would need for my new school.

They took us to live in Japan for a month. It happened to be the month right after I graduated from high school. While my friends were basking in the sun on their graduation trips, I was plugging my nose trying to keep from throwing up while gagging down the sushi some sweet Japanese neighbors offered us.

My parents were wise. They knew in the end these things would create memories my siblings and I would cherish forever and bring us closer as a family. They taught us that "hard is good" and that we'd appreciate all this in the long run.

And they were right.

To this day, camping brings back the greatest memories. I look back on our month-long camping trip with such fond emotions. The stories around the campfire. The spring that was our "refrigerator." The trips to town (two hours away) to restock groceries and to take a shower at the local swimming pool. The challenge of trying to make my beloved chocolate chip cookies in an old wood-burning stove we somehow lugged into camp.

In England I came out of my shy shell. I learned more than I ever knew I could. I was stretched in so many ways as we traveled around going to art museums and neighboring countries. I grew so close to my family.

I'm so thankful for the understanding I gained in Japan. We were exposed to a new culture, and I got a taste for my newfound obsession with traveling.

All these memories turned from being something we complained and carried on about into things that not only made us stronger and better but brought us closer as a family. Our ties were made much stronger as we struggled and learned together. Our lives were enriched.

Now as I have my own little tribe of people to teach that "hard is good," I think of my wise parents when I tell my kids we're trying something new. Even something as small as going to a museum or on a drive to a neighboring town can cause a serious uproar of complaints. They want to play with friends. They want my husband and me to leave them happily to their Wii and the DVD player. But I smile to myself as they remind me of my own younger self, and I tell them tough luck, we're doing it anyway.

Even the smallest memories make all the difference.

A couple of months ago we went hiking. Yep, to that whining and complaining tune I loaded the kids in the car.

And these are some of the things that happened:

I lugged thirty-one-pound Lucy in a backpack up and down rocky terrain for four miles. In flip-flops.

Claire got blisters on both feet but was still pretty tough until she fell on a prickly cactus and got tons of hair-like slivers in her hand. It was all downhill after that.

Max about died because he needed to go to the bathroom so bad and was embarrassed to go in the bushes.

Elle about died because she too needed to go to the bathroom so bad . . . luckily so bad that she had no qualms about going behind a bush.

Dave got stuck at work and couldn't come along.

Lucy decided from her view on my back that my ears looked like great toys. She scratched them to smithereens. And then went for my neck.

Grace fell and scraped her knee.

The list of mishaps goes on. Yeah, I know, it doesn't sound fun. But I've found that you appreciate the good stuff even more when you have the bad stuff to compare it to. And, despite the crazy stuff, you're still creating memories you're all going to remember. Maybe the crazy stuff is really what makes the very best memories.

Although Lucy was darn heavy, I loved hearing her babble away so sweetly in my scraped up ears. She felt the need to give me the sweetest little pats on my shoulder every so often, melting my heart each time.

Max and Elle, lately too busy with their own different friends to hang out together much, stuck together, scrambling up ahead of everyone and happily climbing up nearby boulders and exploring. I loved watching them together.

My sister-in-law drove with me and patiently carried on a full-on conversation with me, completely un-phased by Lucy's screaming. I love moms.

I got to be with my kids. And they got me to be "theirs" for a little while.

And guess what? I think they liked it!

If I don't push to make time to make memories like this, our life becomes the same every day—they play with their friends, and I keep up the house and do my projects. I adore these sweet children I get to hang with—skinned knees, whining, fighting, and all. They better brace themselves, because I'm gonna create as many memories as I can—and I bet they'll thank me for it in the long run!

FAMILY LAWS

Linda

When our first two little girls were three and two, we started a list of family laws in a family meeting. As I remember, we sort of opened it up to nominations for family laws. Our oldest, Saren, knew exactly what the first law should be: Never hit other little girls! We thought it was perfect. Our little two-year-old chirped in, "Never pud in puds" (plug in plugs). What well-trained children we had!

We kept adding to our list of family laws for about five years. When something came up that needed correcting, we added it to the list of family laws. Finally, at about age eight, Saren came to me one day and said, "Mom we have thirty-two family laws! I just can't remember all of them! Even in the whole Bible there are only *ten* commandments. Can't we simplify them a little?"

Of course, we realized immediately that she was exactly right. Kids need simple ideas in order to make them work. We cut the laws down to the bone and decided on five one-word laws with a consequence attached to each one. We even composed a simple song that included repeating the laws over and over again. We sang the song regularly at our family meetings. It was a cheesy little song, but every child could sing it, and those words rang in their brains as they were deciding whether or not to do the right thing.

Every family will have different laws, but our five—each of which we'll outline briefly here—were peace, respect, order, asking, and obedience. We had the children vote on them and help

us figure out a consequence for breaking each of the laws. It was hysterical to listen to the children come up with punishments for broken laws. Since they never thought for a minute that they would break the laws, they said things like, "Put us in our rooms for two days with only bread and water."

In the end, though, the punishments were not severe, just natural consequences. If they broke the law of peace, they went to the repenting bench (see the secret on Arguments for details on that). If they broke the law of respect, they were asked to "start over" when they said something disrespectful. They knew that if their dad or I heard something disrespectful come out of their mouths—which I'm sorry to say occurred quite often—we would say, "Hey, let's start over." That was the trigger phrase to help them realize that what they said was not appropriate and that they would have to keep rephrasing their original statement until they got it right. Sometimes it took five times or more; but it usually worked!

For example, if we asked a child to take out the garbage, he might yell, "Why do you always ask me to do stuff just when I'm in the middle of a TV show? Why don't you ask someone else?" A disrespectful answer such as that would be followed with, "Let's start over on that!" By about the third time, the child might realize what he could have said that would be better. Maybe something like, "I'm watching my favorite TV show right now. Is it OK if I take it out as soon as it's over?" This requires practice, but it's a great secret to help kids work out suitable responses.

Our "asking" law was pretty self-explanatory: kids should always ask before they go somewhere. The punishment was a natural consequence: the next time the child wanted to go somewhere, the answer would be no. Consistent follow-through was the only hard part of this family law!

The "order" law is explained a little more fully in the secret on Order. But you should know that we tried a hundred different ways to get our kids to be responsible with their things; this was a hard law to follow! We made it fun by using a Gunny Bag (explained in the secret on Order).

8349 0000897

0000897 8349

Sell your books at
sellbackyourBook.com!

Go to sellbackyourBook.com
and get an instant price
quote. We even pay the
shipping - see what your old
books are worth today!

We tried putting everything left out on the floor on top of their beds. Richard thought that would make it impossible to go to bed until they put things away, but he was wrong about that. It didn't bother them at all. At one point I charged them money for each thing I had to put in their rooms, and then we used the "booty" for treats for our family meetings. I even went on strike once and didn't pick up *anything* for three days. It was a great eye-opener for all of us! Every family will have a different plan for implementing order in the home, but the important thing is that your kids know that order is important in your family!

Breaking our last law, the law of obedience, meant a time out in their room. Like our other rules, we outlined how obedience worked in a family meeting. Basically, we decided that when a parent said, "Please," the children had to be obedient.

Of course, every family will have different ways to make family laws work. We have a friend who owns a granite and marble shop. He claims that his kids didn't pay much attention to the family laws until he had them engraved on marble and hung in the front hall. Do whatever works!

Even though kids don't always realize it, they love to have boundaries. Family laws help them know what is expected of them and show them that you love them so much you want to protect them! A few simple rules will improve your offense more than you ever imagined.

PART 3

ANALYZE

. . . how to make things better

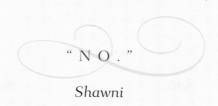

"NO."

Shawni

Sometimes one of the biggest secrets of parenting is to learn to analyze how we deal with our children and to say "no" every once in a while. Even when what we really want is to say "yes!" We want so much to give our kids what we can. We want to make them happy. But the most well-adjusted kids know how do deal with life when it throws them a "no."

Recently I had an interesting discussion with a dad who was at the park with his three-year-old daughter. We know their family and I was glad to have a minute to pick his brain about parenting. They have five kids, and the youngest (who was there at the park with him) was a little bit of a surprise. There's a big gap between this little girl and her next older sibling. I've been curious as to how that little girl is so darn well adjusted. Although she has four much older siblings who must obviously dote on her like crazy, she doesn't seem to be spoiled at all. I contrast her to my number five . . . well, I'll just say there are a few differences. This dad told me something interesting. He said the trick is to hold firm on saying "no" and stick with it when you need to. Don't give in. Don't relax just because you have so much else going on with the older kids that you just don't have time or energy to deal with the screaming and complaining that comes when you stick to your guns.

Well, we mothers know that it's a little harder than you think it will be to stick to your guns when it's your own child lying there on the floor of the grocery store kicking and screaming for something you don't want to give in to. And as you sit there frantically trying to figure out how to leave the store without breaking the eardrums of everyone else there, it's pretty tempting to just give in and buy the darn push pop for some peace and quiet.

After talking to this dad, I sat and analyzed how I deal with my kids. I thought about how Lucy will scream for something and my husband and I will beg the other kids to just give her whatever she wants to save us all from a wild tantrum. I thought about how my kids will ask over and over again for something they want . . . things like a cookie before dinner or a late-night with a friend when they're clearly too tired to play. I thought about how my firm "Wait until after dinner" or "Tonight is not a good night for us" gets weaker and weaker each time they ask until I give in. I realized I have some work to do because it's really a disservice to kids to just continually give them what they want. I've realized that the key is to take time out to talk to my kids about why I'm saying no and then hold firm, or with little kids, to distract them and get them interested in something else.

The world is full of no's . . . no, you can't skip work on a whim; no, you can't buy that big screen TV that's beyond your budget; no, you can't eat to your hearts' content every day and expect to lose weight. It's so important for kids to learn early that "no" is an answer they're going to get from time to time in their lives, and they better learn to deal with it. They need to learn delayed gratification. We value things we have to work and wait for.

Sure, getting what they want makes kids happy and often helps them behave, at least for a few minutes. But by giving in to continual requests we deny our kids (and ourselves) the great lessons to be learned by delayed gratification. I mean, seriously, what happened to waiting until Christmas for that most coveted big toy? What happened to saying "no" to expensive sports and music lessons that take away from family time? Why do we sometimes find it so tough to explain to our kids that they can't just have everything their hearts desire?

So I've taken what this wise dad said to heart. And I think it's a serious motherhood secret that kids feel more secure when they have limits and don't always get what they want . . . when they have to work for things and wait for things.

After all this "no" business though, it's important to realize that another motherhood secret is "yes!" There's a lot of room in life for yes. The other day as I was sitting working on something on the computer two of my girls came in asking if they could give me a manicure. Well, a manicure was the absolute last thing on my mind . . . I was in the middle of a million things that needed to get done. But I stopped and told them yes. I let them work their magic on my nails and boy howdy, you should have seen the looks of delight on their faces because of it. There are so many things we definitely should say yes to, even when we're tempted to say no. But sometimes what will bring more happiness in the long run is to say "no" once in a while . . . and stick with it!

CHANGE

Linda

One secret I wish I'd known earlier is that most of the time when you want change, it's *you* that has to change first. There is one thing I wish I would have changed about myself while my children were growing up. I wish I hadn't hated Halloween! Every year on about October 1, the kids started thinking about wanting to be werewolves, witches, wizards, princesses, pirates, and pancakes for Halloween. The costume-gathering process included trips to craft stores, drug stores, grocery stores, and Deseret Industries to hunt down gypsy costumes, Dracula teeth, fake blood, and pom poms. All that, along with the inevitable last-minute "Mom, I changed my mind, I want to be a wedding cake" made smoke come out of my ears!

Exhausted and muttering under my breath the morning after, as I washed the "blood" off of the counter and the black hairspray off the mirror, I would begin resenting the task of getting rid of the three pounds of Halloween candy sitting just below my waist. I was already dreading having to do it all over again next year!

But I have changed! Maybe because now it's my children who are doing all the running around instead of me! I love the creativity and seeing the joy in my grandchildren's eyes as pictures are sent from far and wide of each adorable child pretending to be something or somebody else!

There are so many things in our life that we want to change. Maybe a husband is not as appreciative or pro-active as we wish. Maybe he is too strong-willed or oblivious to our needs.

Perhaps a child is so totally opposite from the way we wish they were (more like us) that we can barely tolerate their behavior. Sometimes we wish our circumstances were different, that we had more money, more time, more stuff.

All of those things are nearly impossible for us to change. All you really can change is yourself! A great exercise in change is to figure out how to respond to irritating and aggravating behavior in a different way and not let frustrating behavior upset you.

Analyze the situation! First write down the things that are driving you crazy about your husband and/or your children, mother-in-law, or even a neighbor. Actually make a little grid. Write things that bother you about your most important relationships on one side. Then leave two blank spaces. In the first, write how you react when that bothering behavior occurs. Next analyze how you could react differently to that annoyance. This is a lot harder than it seems on paper, but it is so fun to calculate how to respond differently the next time you are bothered by something in a relationship. Don't plan on it having results overnight. It takes time and concentrated effort, but if you can really pull it off, you will find that through your changes, others will begin to change in their response to you!

Here's an example. Perhaps your child is driving you crazy because she whines incessantly about every little thing. Write this down on a sheet of paper, then analyze how you can change. Resolve to solve the whining problem by changing your response to it. Perhaps you can have a talk with your daughter about how much you want to help her stop whining. Start out by apologizing for your previous reactions and tell her that you promise you won't get mad at her anymore but will just use a simple reminder when she starts whining. Sometimes a secret sign can help, like making a thumbs-down when she starts to whine. If she can stop immediately and speak in a reasoning voice when you give her a thumbs-down, tell her that she can have a reward. Depending on the age of the child, the reward might be a small treat or just a daily mark on a chart with a bigger reward at the end of a week. Be consistent; don't go back to yelling at her or lecturing her if she doesn't stop whining immediately. Instead, just walk away or establish something else you'll do if the sign doesn't work.

Each thing you want to change about a child or a relationship starts with *you* changing *your* response to what is happening. It's all about analyzing your situation and figuring out how to change to make things better.

In the end, the real secret is not to wait thirty years to change. A relationship is so precious that irritations need to be addressed before your resentments become habits and before you become so ingrained in your responses that it becomes almost impossible to re-route your feelings.

I could have enjoyed Halloween so much more if I had looked at it as a magnificent opportunity for creativity instead of a yearly irritation that could barely be tolerated. I thought I couldn't wait to be able to give the contents of those packed costume drawers to charity. Fortunately I stopped just in time to think about my grandchildren. Today those costume drawers are the most often opened drawers in the house by our next generation. In hindsight, I am so grateful for those Halloween memories. How I wish I had put on a smile and relished those moments sooner!

Change isn't as easy as writing something down on paper. It takes concentrated, dedicated effort, but it's a great secret to help in turning around relationships or stubborn, entrenched ideas so that you don't regret it later.

"WHATEVER"

Shawni

I grew up with stars in my eyes about motherhood. When I envisioned myself as a mother I saw someone who was always dressed, hair done, accessorized, and level-headed. Smeared peanut butter or a splatter of spit up were not really accessories I had in mind. The mother I envisioned always got her kids where they needed to be on time. Her children were perfect, lined in a row, dressed in clean clothes, freshly washed and curled hair gleaming in the sun, each face emblazoned with a glittering smile. They would all listen to their perfect mother's every word with baited breath (I had yet to come in contact with selective listening), and they would instantly obey when she set them to a task.

Well, needless to say being a mother for real has made me drastically change my idea of perfect motherhood.

I've learned that one of the biggest secrets of motherhood doesn't lie in the ability to dress children immaculately or to always be perfectly patient. The secret is to remember what is really important and to actively employ the word "Whatever" to the rest.

There was one particular night when I realized that *whatever* should become a precious part of every mother's vocabulary. I was with my kids at Petco. They were roaming the aisles in delight and I had to laugh as I took note of their appearance. I realized I had become the mom I vowed I'd never be: the one who takes her kids out looking like ragamuffins when it's obviously past their bedtime. I used to look at those moms and think, "How can they go out like that? Is it really that hard to brush their hair and wipe down their faces?" I realize now that, yes, sometimes it is that hard.

Let's say your oldest child has a fetish with his favorite Suns basketball jersey—yep, he wears it every day—and also has a bad habit of wiping his dirty hands on his shirt; your fourth child (whose hair is sticking out in every direction from her fourth ponytail re-do of the day) has just leaned over into peanut butter, smearing it on her third clean shirt of the day; your baby has a cold and goopy eyes and you have wiped her poor chubby face so many times it's starting to chafe; your third child has already changed into her pajamas from her swimsuit, forgetting that you are going to the pet store for family home evening. As you finish making the last peanut but-ter sandwiches you're having for dinner (because your husband missed his flight and is still out of town and you don't feel like making anything else), you realize that if you don't leave right then the store will close and the hopes of your oldest two children—who have been begging for a pet ever since Grandpa gave them money to buy one (without asking their parents first)—will be crushed if you don't make it to the store before closing time. So what can you do besides load those sticky, straggly-haired kids in the car and head out to the pet store in all your splendid "good mom" glory?

As we walked those aisles I'm sure other customers had the same thoughts my young, single self had many years ago: "Wow, those are some raggedy kids!" But I took a deep look at each one of them—unruly hair, pajamas, dirt, and all—and thought, *whatever,* and loved them even more as I watched them oooo and ahhhhhh over the fish, gerbils, and snakes.

In spite of myself, that perfect mom I dreamed of being has gone by the wayside. Instead I'm the mother who realizes after she scrambles to get everyone to her son's baseball game that she has forgotten her own shoes and ends up tip-toeing around on her seven-year-old's extra pair of flip-flops all night.

I'm the mom trying to keep all my kids together and out of harm's way as we maneuver ourselves through the mall to the new double-decker carousel, the kids' faces smeared with their leftover chocolate Frosties from our drive-thru run and all of us plugging our noses because Lucy is stinky and I forgot to bring a spare diaper.

I'm even the mom who sometimes allows her kids to eat chocolate chip cookies for breakfast because that's what I want, too.

So the secret is, say "Whatever" . . . and say it a lot. Life is crazy as a mother. You have to pick your battles carefully. There are some things that are essential to ingrain into these precious minds. Children need to know we love them unconditionally. They need to know they can trust us. They need to feel safe. But the minutia of life? I say, "Whatever." As long as the important stuff is intact, I'm good with that!

BE YOUR OWN KIND OF "BEST MOM"

Shawni

Sometimes I try to become what I call a "Library Mom." You know, those have-it-all-together moms at the library who speak in hushed tones to their kids as they usher them around, helping them find appropriate books. They check out a huge stack and always return the books on time. I also categorize some of the great moms I see at the doctor's office, the ones who bring a bag full of age-appropriate learning things to do with their kids while they wait, and as they play with their kids they softly explain to them their plans for the rest of the day: "We'll be here at the doctor for just a little longer and then we get to go to the grocery store. Then we'll go home and read all your library books!"

These moms are pretty much the opposite of the usual me. I'm the mom who's racing through the library trying to keep up with her kids while juggling her baby and a stack of books on her hip as her kids are twirling around, yelling in excitement about the books they're tearing off the shelves. I'm also the mom at the doctor's office who's trying to keep one eye on her kids while trying to catch up on reading her book club book with the other eye. And don't even get me started about what happens at the grocery store. Yep, I'm the mom who's trying to keep from crying herself as her kids whine and beg for gum and fruit snacks and chocolate while I try to check out—and suddenly realize I forgot something very important that's in the back corner of the store.

Although I put that Library Mom on a pedestal I have realized that I'm not her, and that's OK. It's taken a while, but I've also learned that many of the Library Moms I used to envy probably have their fair share of not-so-glowing moments with their children, too. In fact one day a while ago I had a little epiphany about it.

It was a day when my girls and I had a serious plan. Dave was out of town with our older two kids, so Grace, Claire, Lucy, and I packed up the double stroller, clicked on Gracie's bike helmet, and headed out for a four-mile run to the library. The plan was to check out books, listen to story time, and I'd be a Library Mom for the afternoon.

Well, we never actually made it *into* the library; but I did return two books that were two months overdue in the drive-thru book return as we ran. We took a break to take in the beauty of the horses and the strange emu and four nice dogs on the way. We stopped at the riparian preserve behind the library and fed the ducks. Then the girls wanted to stay and play. So I sat there with them and hung out in the gorgeous weather. Suddenly it didn't seem to matter that we were missing story time and the other Library Mom things I had planned.

While the older girls played to their hearts' content, I worked with Lucy on recognizing each of her sisters and showing me where her nose is. On the way home we looked for signs of spring and gathered a whole armful of wild flowers to bring home with us. I was compassionate both times Grace fell off her bike and howled like she was going to die because of a tiny scrape. I may not have been the Library Mom I had always longed to be, but I was the kind of mom my kids needed that day. And it felt good.

That afternoon I bribed the girls to help me clean out and re-organize all the winter and summer clothes. Grace worked so hard she earned a mini-pedicure, and you should have seen the excitement oozing out of her as her toenails were painted bright, glittery blue with white flowers. Claire didn't work so hard, but I was able to let her know that next time she'd be picking out some sparkly nail polish, too, if she worked her little heart out like Gracie did; and not even one tantrum resulted from my explanation.

Later we had a big dance party with root beer floats before I tucked them into bed. It was magical. I was my own kind of Library Mom that day. Yes, I did forget the sunscreen, which resulted in one of poor Lucy's large cheeks being sun kissed; and yes, only two out of three of the girls got their hair done that day, but Grace did proclaim me to be the best mom in the world . . . three times. Now that feels good.

Most days I'm flying by the seat of my pants, but each day that I really put my heart into it I think I come a little closer to being the mom I want to be. I want to be the best kind of mom *I* can be. The secret isn't to try to be the best mom I see in so many others. It's to analyze what my own strengths are, to build on them, and to apply what I know to my parenting. That way I become my *own* kind of "best mom." And that's what my kids need me to be.

NUMBER ONE

Linda and Shawni

Linda: There are so many fabulous mothers in the world! I have seen their resilience, their creativity, their undying devotion to the quest of helping their children become the very best they can be. I know their devotion to their cause and I know that nothing deters them from thinking of inspiring ways to help struggling children.

But *sometimes* I think we are better mothers than we are wives. I may be the leader in this fallacy. I remember clearly saying to Richard after the birth of our ninth child and after finding his dishes left around the house, "Richard, I have nine children and I really don't think I can have *ten* children! *You* have got to take care of *yourself!*"

I was right about his needing to put away dishes but dead wrong in thinking that he had to take care of himself. My very first priority, even if it doesn't mean equal time, is loving my husband and nurturing that relationship through all the pandemonium of living that goes on at our house.

You should know that we have spent most of our lives since we met arguing about how things should be done. We each look at situations, solve problems, and organize ourselves in entirely different ways. Both of us are strong willed and certain that our way is right. He sees the big picture while I work on the details.

One Sunday we decided to write down three things we thought we needed from the other and three things we thought the other needed from us. Then we traded papers. What a fun exercise! We laughed about how we could still see things so differently after all these years and yet we took stock of what we could each do to fulfill the needs of the other more effectively.

Through the years I have figured that the kids are only in our home for a finite number of years (for us that number seemed infinite) and after that, what we have left at the house is our relationship with each other (as well as the continuing bigger, more urgent needs of the children as they spin off into their own worlds outside our home). By then this relationship with each other is even more important as we go forward together.

We know there are probably a lot of single moms reading this book, and we salute you. Your job is the hardest job in the world. But for those of you who have husbands living and working with you, learning to prioritize your "number one" may be one of the most important things you will do as you craft and create your family.

Shawni and Dave have one of the finest relationships I know. It is full of give and take; serious disagreements are usually resolved with good humor. You can tell, just by being around them for a few minutes, that they like each other . . . a lot! Here is what she has to say about her "number one" and that all-important relationship.

Shawni: Sometimes I miss Dave. We live in the same house, sleep in the same bed, sit at the same table for dinner, and raise the same kids. But sometimes, when things get really crazy, it's like we're strangers passing each other in the hallway with ringing headaches from screaming kids.

On a typical evening as we try to talk, me asking what he has on the agenda for the weekend and he telling me some story that happened at work, Grace is interrupting to tell me (in a very dramatic way) every detail from her field trip, Lucy's screaming for who-knows-what since she's so darn frustrated that she can't tell us, Claire's crying in the corner because she got her feelings hurt about something or other, Max is pounding on the piano, and Elle's begging for a friend to stay for dinner.

Oh, and then there are the friends causing commotion, too: playing tag, which involves running around the house either slamming the doors or leaving them wide open (great for the air conditioning bill); needing supervision while swimming; fighting over who gets which princess dress-up . . . you get the idea. Oh, and let's not forget about the incessant ringing of that darn phone. (We don't usually answer our phone, but the ringing alone causes a little bit of head ringing.)

I love being a mother with all my heart—commotion and all. I love to kiss those kids' cheeks and snuggle up to read bedtime stories together. But as much as I adore those kids, Dave is my "number one." My sweetheart. My lover. My best friend. And when I'm a shriveled up little old lady (as little as you can shrink to when you start out at six feet tall), I want to remember this: he was my first priority. He's the one who lights up my heart with something as little as giving me a wink across the dinner table commotion. He's the one I'd rather be with than anyone else in the world.

Take time to analyze your relationship with your spouse. How can you make it better, more fun, more consistent, more "number one"? Make "dating" him a priority . . . even if you've been married for twenty years. Doing so will make all the difference, and is, perhaps, one of the most important secrets of motherhood.

PASSION

Shawni

Mothers need to have their own passions. Yes, yes, motherhood is a passion. Doting on our kids and really *knowing* them and helping them through life is certainly a passion to be proud of. But we also need to branch out and find other things we're interested in—for our own sakes as well as for our kids'.

I love to read. I love to be sucked into different worlds as I delve into a good book. Books take me to places I've never been and make me think about things outside my little realm of changing diapers and dusting blinds and hugging my kids to smithereens. I want so much to be open to the bigger world . . . to see outside my little bubble here at home, and I want my kids to see that too. Books do that for me.

I love for my kids to see me reading. When I'm in crunch time for my book club they always want to know what's going on in my book. I love explaining things to them and telling them the story as they sit spellbound by my book summary. I love that each time they see me reading after I start the story, they want to hear an update on what's happening next. A lot of times when they see me cramming they'll pull out their books, too, and come sit by me for a little impromptu read-a-thon.

Motherhood is the most important career we can put our energy into. But it's important to find other things to balance us out and help complete us. I'm not talking about things that take us away from mothering. I'm talking about things that show our kids that we are interested in the world, too. Things like getting a good education. Things like delving into and analyzing the scriptures. Things like caring about serving in the community. And once we find our passions we need to share them with our kids.

Lately my kids have begged to have me teach them a thing or two about my camera. (I'd be fascinated by something I saw hanging around my mother's neck on a continual basis, too!) I love the time we spend together doing photography. It bonds us. It helps them understand me more. It helps them realize that they, too, need to have their own passions, and that those passions can enrich their lives. Their passions may end up being vastly different from my passions . . . or they may be just the same. The important thing is that they have them. Passions complete us and make us into more balanced people. They give us depth and drive.

I am a wife and a mother first and foremost. But I am also a photographer. I am also a reader. I am also a friend. I am also a traveler. And I'm glad my kids know it.

ORDER

Linda

I have no idea where this abundantly forwarded e-mail originated from, but a friend sent it to me a couple years ago, and I love it! To paraphrase, it tells the story of a dad coming home from work to find a veritable disaster. Outside doors were left open, kids were still in their pajamas, and the dog was nowhere to be found. Toothpaste was on the walls of the bathrooms, toilets were not flushed, and miles of toilet paper were unrolled on the floor. The fridge door was open, and cartoons blared through the house, though no one was watching. The sink and counters were piled high with dishes; berry stains from breakfast were still on the counter. The dad rushed into every bedroom, where none of the beds were made, trying to find his wife and thinking something terrible must have happened. He finally found her in their bedroom, reading a book. With disbelief he exclaimed, "What in the world happened?" She looked up calmly and with a smile said, "Every day when you get home from work you ask what on earth I do all day, so today I didn't do it!"

Every mother of children has to smile as we identify with the literally hundreds of things we do every day that go unnoticed unless we *don't* do them: the dusting, the mopping, the washing, the bed making, the dish doing, the sweeping, and the cleaning up of never-ending messes! Some days when all nine of our children were home I remember thinking that my hands had probably touched literally a thousand different things in one day. Keeping a house in order is one of the most frustrating realities of being a mother—maybe second only to two-year-old tantrums.

Through my travels, I've realized that when it comes to order, the wealthy families of the world are living a different life than the average American mom. They have drivers who take kids to classes and lessons, cooks who provide lovely meals, and child caregivers who feed the children and care for their everyday needs.

"Ah, what a life!" you might say; yet, in balance, consider this: some of them also have to deal with arranged marriages, living with constant scrutiny from the press, and sometimes even driving in armored cars and hiring bodyguards for each child to prevent the all-too-prevalent kidnappings for ransom. All things considered, I'd take my own do-it-yourself life . . . except for the bit about the maid who always keeps things in order.

In those old days, with a house bursting with children, no matter how organized or determined I was to keep things in order, there was always something about order that was *not* in order! I have gone through different phases with this problem. First I tried to comfort myself with the old saying, "Cleaning house while kids are growing is like shoveling walks when it's still snowing." I tried to let things go; but the clutter was so hard to live amongst! In frustration with the chaos, I also realized that "Thing order precedes thought order." Some days I felt as though it was certainly true that "Of all the things I'd lost, I missed my mind the most!"

Keeping things in order is a constant struggle. I've come to realize that there are stages of mothering when order is nice but not entirely possible or even absolutely necessary to our happiness. Sometimes we just have to smile, selectively neglect things, and try to enjoy the chaos! Here are ideas for maintaining just a little more order for each child-age-group:

Preschoolers: Get a laundry bag. Draw on eyes and a nose and use the drawstring for a mouth. Introduce the laundry bag as "Gunny Bag," who lives in the attic (or a closet) and swoops down unannounced, *starving* for left-out toys and clothes. He eats them and then goes back to the attic until Saturday when he "regurgitates" them so the child can retrieve his toys and clothes. If Gunny Bag gets an item twice, though, the item goes off to the charity store! The kids will have

a love-hate relationship with Gunny Bag when you put your hand behind your ear, survey the mess, and say, "I think I hear Gunny Bag coming!" The ensuing scramble to clean up is fun to behold!

Elementary Age: This is one of about eighty-five ideas we used through the years that worked pretty well. Put a basket in the kitchen and drop anything left out in the basket. The only way to get an item back is for the child to pay for it out of his own money. You decide on the amount. It could be anything from twenty-five cents to a dollar depending on the number of children you have and the amount you want to have by the next week when you use the money to chip in for a fun family activity.

Teenagers: Tell teens that you don't give a darn about the way their room looks during the week as long as something doesn't fall out at you when you open the door. But remind them that they will not be going out on the weekend until their room is clean. That everyday nagging just isn't worth putting your relationship on the rocks!

There are literally hundreds of things to try as you work to instill order. You may have to try a good many of them to find one that works. We found we had to change ideas periodically to keep order fresh in the kids' minds. Don't get discouraged. Remind yourself that loving your kids is really the most important thing, and that order isn't always necessary. Good luck!

ATTITUDE

Shawni

Sometimes I think I'm losing it. Usually that feeling comes on a day like this: Morning breaks with Claire wetting her bed—again. Lucy's diaper explodes during breakfast. It's a half-day at school, which my sweet children directly translate into meaning a five-hour party with everyone they can think of in the neighborhood—at our house—to which I, of course, say yes. Yep, I say yes, even though I happen to have a headache and have just cleaned the whole house. The day progresses with me cringing as all my hard work disappears when the kids traipse in and out of the house, wet from the pool and spilling popcorn and juice box drips in little trails behind them. The slamming doors and teasing and rough-housing don't do much for my headache. And then comes the rush of carpool time, and then dinnertime, and then sweet Elle crams the brimming-full-of-sparkly-clean-dishes dishwasher even more full . . . with really dirty ones. Lucy falls off the table and has a fifteen-minute meltdown, and Claire decides she needs to pout and cry about everything from a stern look I gave her to the fact that she couldn't get Lucy to laugh. So by the time I send them all off to get on their pajamas after Dave leaves for a meeting, and I open the dryer with more laundry waiting to be folded, I am ready for my own meltdown.

This is when I must remind myself that a lot of worse things could have happened. And a lot of good things *did* happen: I got to go to Max's class and talk about art, which we both love. Dave even stayed home with the little girls while I was gone so I didn't have to find someone else to watch them. A friend picked Lucy, Claire, and me up in the morning and we had a lot of fun with her and her daughters at "transportation day" at preschool. Elle prepared the night's dinner at her cooking class the previous night, and it was delicious after simply cooking in the Crock-Pot all day. My friend drove the tennis carpool for me. It should have been a smooth day. But it wasn't.

I guess what makes me frustrated is that I realize days like the one just described—yes, it all happened in the same, real day—was tough because of me and my attitude. I'm the mother, and because of that, I had the power to make a day like this one better. My attitude makes a difference. And it's not a little difference. It's big. It's huge. It can change the outcome of an entire day. Of course we can't always be "on." We can't always have great little ideas for our kids that we explain in a cheerful way. Sometimes we just have an awful day. But when we can muster up a good attitude, it sure makes a difference!

Let's look at an example: Say my four-year-old tries to pour a fresh pitcher of lemonade into her little flimsy paper cup and misses, resulting in the entire contents of the pitcher (sticky lemonade) covering the counter, the cabinets, and the floor (of course, it's a freshly cleaned floor). We've all been faced with this same scenario, right? Kids for some reason are mesmerized by doing things by themselves and being independent. Since I've had quite a few opportunities for experimenting on how I would react to a situation like this (spilling drinks is a very regular occurrence around our house), I know that my attitude makes all the difference. If I calmly have the perpetrator help me clean up the mess and tell them sweetly that maybe next time the pitcher is that full they could ask me for help, the result is a happy child, a happy mother (I've spent some quality time with my child explaining something, and that always makes me happy), and a clean kitchen. If I start huffing and puffing and raving on and on about how I try so hard to keep things clean and no one helps out and I always have to clean up after everyone (yep, I'm embarrassed to admit I've taken that route, too), it results in a poor child with cheeks covered in crocodile tears, a very frustrated mother, and a bunch of stickiness. My attitude makes all the difference in the atmosphere of our home.

So my rule of thumb is that motherhood is made up of both the good and the bad. Crazy things happen every single day, but that's what I signed up for. The secret is that if I remember to take a deep breath every time there's a catastrophe and analyze the situation before I react, it makes all the difference. Easier said than done, right? But I'll add another little secret: the old adage of counting to ten when on the verge of explosion works wonders.

PART 4

KIDS ARE LIKE PUZZLES

. . . how to make the pieces fit together

WHO IS THIS KID ANYWAY?

Linda

As far as I'm concerned, one of the silliest bits of "wisdom" ever imparted to parents goes like this: "Children are like lumps of clay, and parents are the sculptors." This leads parents to believe that with the proper time and influence children can be shaped into whatever parents would like them to be. So not true!

I'd rather think of children as seedlings. Even though tiny seedlings look very similar as they sprout, in the end they will become who they are. Some will produce flowers—sunflowers, delphiniums, or snapdragons. Some will produce fruits—apples, oranges, and, yes, even lemons. But they are who they are. A sunflower can't be changed to an apple no matter how hard you try! The secret to how well each little seedling grows to become its best self depends on the gardener giving it the appropriate light, water, fertilizer, and love.

As mothers, when our babies are first placed in our arms at birth, we are overwhelmed with the joy and magic of the precious bundle joining our family. I like the way Anne Morrow Lindbergh describes it: "In the sheltered simplicity of the first days after a baby is born, one sees again the magical closed circle, the miraculous sense of two people existing only for each other, the tranquil sky reflected on the face of the mother nursing her child" (*Gift from the Sea*, 67).

Time passes, as does babyhood, toddlerhood, and those years when two- and three-year-olds sometimes drive us over the edge. Our children aren't who we thought they would be. They don't respond to the world as we sometimes wish. Problems arise as we realize that they are not us! As they grow older, and we think they should learn to be responsible, they still can't remember to put their socks in the hamper, let alone do their jobs! They develop weird quirks and unruly behavior and are sometimes even disrespectful!

After every parenting speech Richard and I give, we are attacked by a group of parents who are frustrated with a child. They want their child to be more manageable, more "normal." In probing deeper, we usually find that they are just dealing with an individual who they haven't yet figured out. Over and over we remind parents that the little person they are frustrated with *is who he is* . . . so figure it out and deal with it!

Of course, there are things we can do to help that child on his or her way; but in the end, our biggest responsibility is to watch and pray. We need to *watch* our children with the specific intent of seeing who they really are and *pray* like crazy that we can give them what they need to succeed! What a challenge it is for us to try to figure out what makes children happy, sad, frustrated, delighted! Who are they really? When we figure that out and accept it, it is crucial to provide the necessary water, light, fertilizer, and love to help each child become who he is meant to be, especially if it isn't what we had in mind!

After years of lying awake nights worrying that I had a prima-ballerina inside one of my children that would never be discovered (since I know nothing about dance), I have realized—and this is a great secret—that children will naturally gravitate to their passions if they are given fertile soil and the encouragement they need to become who they really are.

Looking at our grown children and their own passions has made me realize that there is no way I could have figured out exactly what they would develop passions for! I have no understanding of photography myself, but somehow a majority of our children have developed a passion for it. I did know from the time they were two that some would be fabulous salesmen and entrepreneurs; but I had no idea just how that would play out. I believed one child could easily organize the world if the world would just permit it. And some of my children have a deep passion for service. Those children all grew up in the same environment with the same parents (although the older ones had an entirely different experience than the younger "spoiled" ones). Yet the spectrum of their interests and passions is incredible!

Our son Josh is a brilliant computer whiz. He instinctively knew how to work the intricacies of a computer from the first moment he saw one. I call him with my computer woes, and he patiently helps me find our lost documents while I'm crying on the other end of the phone. He fixes my computer from Arizona. But despite his technological talents, what he has always really wanted to do is work with kids. When he first brought up the idea as he entered college, we recognized that he did have an amazing rapport with kids, so we patted him on the back and suggested that he get a degree in construction management and then work with kids as a volunteer. Sure enough, he got a degree with honors in construction management and is now one of the best third grade teachers who ever lived! He teaches at a charter school in Arizona and is changing the lives of the children he teaches. His passion for giving them a great education is nothing less than remarkable. It is especially delightful for us to watch him as a teacher, because as a child he was totally irresponsible, couldn't remember to do his homework, and if he did actually did do it one night, he couldn't remember to take it back to school with him the next day. Ah, what goes around comes around!

In the process of raising our children, I have found that some children really do need more sleep than others. Some need more praise and reinforcement than others. Some like help from every angle, and others would rather just do their own thing. Our child who was so right-brained that it took many years of special training to help him to learn to read, the one who I thought would never make it through college, not only graduated with flying colors but has become a "learning expert." He sets and accomplishes amazing goals, listens to motivational books, biographies, and historical novels on tape while he drives long miles in his car and is a top salesman on the East coast. Who would have known? The child who was most whiny now has a whiner of her own. The one who never thought she had any friends is organizing the mothers of the world through retreats for moms who want to make motherhood their most important career. The one who gave us a run for our money on curfews is now a fabulous father.

Of course, appropriate limits need to be placed to help curb disrespect and willful bad behavior. But sometimes parents need to recognize that those behaviors can come from an insecurity of which we're not yet aware or from a lack of communication and understanding. That's the rub! Figuring it out is one of our greatest responsibilities as mothers. No two children are ever exactly the same. Figuring out those differences and capitalizing on them is one of the greatest challenges of motherhood! Remember to have fun in the process! As Mark Twain said, "My mother had a great deal of trouble with me, but I think she enjoyed it."

The secret is that you never know what that cry-baby, argumentative, learning disabled child will become, so just keep watching and praying, fertilizing and weeding. And more often than not, magic will happen!

REAL LIFE

Shawni

My husband and I are worriers. We worry about everything. Most of the time the things we worry about are a little different. I worry about things like whether we may have hurt someone's feelings by leaving a party and not saying good-bye (Dave laughs at that one) and what sort of emotional turmoil may be going on inside one of our kid's heads (when in reality they are most likely plugging along completely happy-go-lucky). Dave worries more about things like shipments from China for his business and making sure that he has TiVoed every football game known to man. But the bottom line is that we are both total worriers. So our baby, Lucy, makes us worry.

First of all, she was born with six toes on one foot (which we've since realized is more common than we thought). Then we noticed a little strawberry hemangioma on her head. Then another one popped up on her cheek. Each of these things in and of itself was fine. We had her sixth toe removed without much trauma (except that we still kind of miss it!). And strawberry hemangioma birthmarks, according to doctors, are really no big deal. They say that by age five most of them shrink back down and disappear. But aside from those worries we worry about her development. I have four other children. I've watched them each move through every milestone. I know generally what kids should be doing at each different stage. And Lucy's different. Lucy makes us worry.

Chances are we're worrying over nothing, and all the doctor visits and therapies we do with her will put her right back on track. But as I sat in the state-run office for developmental delays one day, waiting for Lucy to get her ears checked, I felt like I was introduced to "real life." I sat watching other parents deal with kids who had much more significant issues than Lucy has, and it suddenly hit me: I lived in a different world with my first four kids. Every one of them hit developmental milestones at the same time. One week they learned to play peek-a-boo. The next maybe they learned to give kisses. Then they started saying words, which were added to one by one, then ten by ten. This was normal. This was life. But with Lucy I have suddenly had to re-think development. Lucy will learn something and then forget it. I've never thought of needing to practice a new skill over and over again to make it stick.

I watched the other parents in that waiting room and thought about what they were going through. I thought of all my totally healthy kids and realized that I'm not thankful enough for health, for the quality of life we live because my kids can run and breathe and jump and talk as they should. We have no oxygen tank to lug around or emergency shots sitting by in case one of them eats a peanut. We don't have any inhalers or wheelchairs or walkers to deal with. My kids run to the bus, play tennis, eat junk food, do flips on the trampoline. I realized I had taken all that for granted.

Lucy is probably fine, but some of those kids in that waiting room probably aren't. And my heart aches for them. And what if Lucy isn't fine? What if there's more to it than a little delay?

I called my sister-in-law who is a speech therapist for advice on my way home and left a message for her. As I said the words "Lucy has qualified for speech therapy," I couldn't help getting a little choked up. This is my baby, and she needs more help than I can give her.

My new version of "real life" makes me cherish and appreciate the little things that much more. A few months ago as I was roaming the aisles of Wal-Mart, Lucy pointed at me and said, "Mama." And for the first time I think she really meant, "You are my mama" instead of just some babbling mumbo jumbo. And I almost started crying right there on aisle twenty-nine next to the can openers and cheese graters.

When we got home she pointed to her baby doll and said "didi" which, when translated, means "baby" or "doggie." (It's really a useful word since it's completely interchangeable and especially because it's one of only two words that complete her vocabulary.) But man those little things made me so happy.

That same day marked the first time I set Lucy down from carrying her in a standing position and she didn't fall over or throw a fit. I know these seem like little things, but to me they're huge milestones.

Now Lucy's qualified for physical and developmental therapy, too, and I've had the toughest time trying to find an opening with a developmental speech therapist. It's rough to get a spot, even when qualified. But that is my new "real life," along with rice milk and gluten-free pretzels; and I'm telling you, it's OK, because it makes me love this little girl even more, if that is humanly possible. I love to concentrate on her and focus on really helping her in any way we can. I love that these sweet therapists can come to our house and teach me how to teach my daughter in a way that I've never thought of before. It's a whole new way of thinking. I love that I can then teach my older kids how to teach our baby. I love to watch them dote over her and cheer her along. To be honest, I can't believe those humongous cheeks haven't been kissed off yet. She's just such a huge blessing to our family. I couldn't be more thankful to share with her my new version of "real life."

The secret is to be thankful for our own version of "real life," whatever it may be, and to realize that we're learning through the ups *and* the downs. Some of us will breeze through motherhood (maybe those Library Moms!), and some of us will deal with tremendous heartbreak. Some days we'll want to give up, and other days our hearts will soar with joy over reaching a new milestone. If we remember to be thankful for the good and the bad, our journey will be that much more rewarding in the long run.

STAGES

Linda

Shakespeare's Jacques in *As You Like It* proclaimed: "All the world's a stage, And all the men and women merely players" (Act II, Scene VII, 139–40). I'd like to add that every child who ever lived is going through some sort of "stage" on that stage as they progress through childhood. There was the writing-on-the-walls stage for our oldest and the thumb-sucking stage that lasted through kindergarten for another.

One sixteen-month-old spent most of his time looking for open bathroom doors so he could climb right *into* the toilet. Most kids are happy just unraveling miles of toilet paper, but this kid was not satisfied until he was sitting *in* the toilet, using the toilet seat for his "inner tube" ring, usually fully dressed—often complete with leather shoes—and making a wonderful toilet-plunger sucking noise with his little bottom. For six months I woke up in horror every morning, wondering which of our children might have forgotten to close a bathroom door. The best part of this story is that years later, I was writing a story about this particular incident in our lives and I couldn't remember which child was the bathroom marauder! I had to call one of the other kids to help me remember that it was Noah. Noah! How could I forget that—something so obvious considering the ark, water and all!

Recently, in preparation for the marriage our youngest son, Eli, one of my biggest jobs was to update "The Book." This is a book that I resolved to do for each of our children to be presented to them when they got married. Each book starts at the child's birth. For Eli I recorded my thoughts at his delivery and contemplated his life as I lay in my hospital bed. As he grew I occasionally wrote about the cute things he did and said and solicited entries from his dad and his grandmothers (his grandfathers had passed on). I was determined to write consistently but often I had to catch up on months and, toward the end, years at a time! As I packed it around to catch up as we traveled that last few weeks before his wedding last year, I realized that the last entry I made had been in 1995! I had slipped pictures in the book over the years as reminders, which helped, but what a drive through memory lane it was to complete his book!

I learned so much about him from reading about his life. There were so many stages I had long since forgotten. There was the night that Richard and I came home, having left our sixteen-year-old-daughter Saren babysitting our little ones, to find a fire engine and an ambulance with flashing lights outside our door. Panicked, we rushed in to find a poison control crew standing over Eli, who had just drunk some of the chemicals from his older brother Josh's chemistry set. Unable to get ahold of us in the pre-cell phone days, Saren had wisely called poison control and they were busy "controlling" the event. By the end of the evening, almost our entire street came in to watch Eli throw up several times in the bathtub, and they cheered as he did! Just as a post-script to that event, the next week Eli drank a bottle of cologne! When we called poison control again, they said that he would be fine but that he might get a little drunk! The next week it was Selsun Blue, and so on. I thought the time would never end when Eli would quit drinking weird stuff! But it did!

Next I remembered how merciless Eli was to Charity, his younger sister, who he never forgave for taking over his long three-year reign as the baby of the family. He teased her mercilessly. As he teased, her shrill scream brought about the exact response he was looking for.

I'm sorry to say to you mothers who are presently dealing with rivaling siblings that it took Eli leaving for college for he and Charity to realize how much they adored each other! Now they love each other with a fierce and loyal love that made it hard for Charity to give Eli away to another woman this year. It was especially hard because she is a missionary in England and wasn't able to be with him for the wedding. Luckily we had a life-size cardboard cutout of her to stand in line with the rest of the kids at the wedding breakfast as they waited to give their tributes to their brother. A sister-in-law read Charity's tribute (that she had e-mailed) from behind the "statue" and this is what she had to say:

"Well, brother, I think we both know perfectly what sibling rivalry is. The beautiful thing is that over the years we have both figured out miraculously and perfectly what sibling adoration is. And on this day of your marriage, I want you to know that I love you with such a unique and real love—a love that withstood all the teasing and taunting and shoving and is now a part of my heart of hearts, a love that I will always treasure and carry with me.

"Thank you for teasing me, for making me tough, for protecting me and supporting me. Thank you for cheering me up, for making me laugh, for having crazy adventures all over the world with me, for apologizing and forgiving and building me up. Thank you for teaching me how to be a missionary, a Christian, and a genuinely good person in so many ways. Thank you for making me who I am. Thank you for being my brother and being my friend. I love you! Charity."

There were many years we thought those words would never come! Truly, life is a stage. So hang in there, moms, and know that the secret is to remember that before long each stage will be just a memory to laugh and/or cry about and also an interesting and vital piece of your child's puzzle that you can learn from as he or she progresses from stage to stage.

YOU ARE THE EXPERT

Shawni

As mentioned in the secret called "Real Life," my baby has some developmental delays. This means that we are on a continual quest to figure out her puzzle and get the right early intervention for her. Our journey to find answers was particularly heart-wrenching during a few months in which several different doctors requested blood work. As I sat there with her in the lab that last time we went, holding her with all my might while she flailed around frantically trying to escape the ominous needle, and then left—tears welling up in my eyes—empty handed after they pricked and prodded her but never got a good draw, I thought to myself, "something has just got to give."

Each time we try a new doctor it happens: I get my hopes up. I gear up, thinking to myself that this one is the one who will have some answers for us. This is the doctor that will make everything clear, tell us what we need to do, give us a prescription to fix everything. But every time I leave I feel my heart sink. No more answers. No more information. Just more questions and more worry.

When the geneticist told us Lucy may have some weird disorder, I came home and looked it up on the Internet and knew right away that's not it. She told us she wants us to do more blood tests but somehow can't get us the lab order.

When the neurologist told us that Lucy's MRI results were normal but there was a small cyst in the brain, I told him the "cyst" was probably her strawberry hemangioma. He looked at his records and told me I was right.

The allergist told me that her crazy break-out in hives and hundreds of red dots all over her body one week and her continual goopy eyes that are sometimes swollen shut in the mornings may be due to something as insignificant as sensitive skin. I'm sorry, but I know he's wrong.

The pediatrician gave me a guilt trip when I told him I didn't want to do vaccinations. But in my heart I feel like we needed to wait.

The secret that I have learned is that the more circles I go in, the more I come to the conclusion that no doctor has the complete answer. No one's going to give me a prescription to fix everything. These doctors may be experts in their own individual fields, but they're not experts on Lucy. I've realized that I'm the expert there. The one and only. I'm with her 24/7. I'm her mother. I adore the air she breathes. I know that she loves bananas more than life itself. I know that she hates being in water. I know the look she gives when she understands but she just wants to act stubborn. I'm the one who sits with her for hours each week while therapists work with her on various new skills. I'm the one whose heart yearns to pick her up in the middle of the night and just snuggle with her (I don't do it—I'm not that crazy—but that doesn't mean I don't want to). I'm the one who, even when she's screaming and throwing her best signature tantrum, feels my heart melt to see those crocodile tears run down those chubby cheeks and fill her long eyelashes with moisture.

I may not be a health expert, but I am her expert. And I'll get to the bottom of this . . . someday. Until then I'll snuggle her up and watch and pray, because I love that girl with all my heart. Someone who loves you that dearly is the best kind of expert to have on your side.

While we were in the thick of dealing with the biggest issues with Lucy, my mom sent me this quote from Anna Quindlen. It fits so perfectly with how I feel about Lucy:

"I remember fifteen years ago poring over one of Dr. Brazelton's wonderful books on child development, in which he describes three different sorts of infants: average, quiet, and active. I was looking for a sub-quiet codicil for an eighteen-month-old who did not walk. Was there something wrong with his fat little legs? Was there something wrong with his tiny little mind? Was he developmentally delayed, physically challenged? Was I insane? Last year he went to China. Next year he goes to college. He can talk just fine. He can walk, too" (*Loud and Clear,* 11).

The more I've gone through these ordeals with Lucy the more I realize this is motherhood. As mothers we may not be parenting experts, but we are the experts for our own kids. We can pore over every parenting book we can get our hands on. We can visit multiple specialists. We can scour the Internet for answers to everything from bed-wetting to how to encourage our kids to come out of their shy shells.

But when it comes down to it, we must realize that we mothers are the experts because we're just that—mothers. No matter how many doctors we go to, we're the ones who know when to slow down and figure problems out on our own. Whether our kids have developmental delays, social insecurities, physical handicaps, or stubborn streaks, we mothers are the ones who know how to best help them. We're the ones who tuck them in bed at night and who know how to comfort them after they've had a bad dream. We know what will push them to get straight A's or to go a whole day without whining. We know when firm action needs to be taken when they're out of line or when a stern look will do the trick.

As mothers we're on a continual quest to be those parenting experts we need to be. How do we teach each child responsibility? How do we teach them to selflessly love others? How do we teach them to serve from their hearts? How do we teach them to do hard things? The tricky thing is that the answer is seldom the same, even for siblings. Each child needs individualized tactics to help him or her find the right path. But we can figure it out if we dig in and put our hearts into it, because we're the moms.

We are mothers. We love our children desperately. Thus, we're the experts who can put our children's puzzles together. And most of the time we need to go with our guts, because most of the time we're right. We've got mother intuition. And that makes us the experts.

I couldn't be more thankful for the challenge.

LOVES

Shawni

My kids love broccoli. They love baked potatoes smothered in so much sour cream you can hardly see the potato. They turn up their noses at fruity desserts. Yes, they're my kids. You can almost tell by the food they like. We're one and the same.

It's a little scary how much we rub off on our kids. But a little exciting too—if only we figure out how to rub off some of the good stuff!

I love art. I mean, I really, really love it. I think my love began through exploring art museums with my mom. She rubbed her love right over to me. Growing up, we had the chance to travel a lot, and my amazing mother took me to art museums all over the world.

I remember one visit in particular. It's not the museum I remember, it's just one painting that's vivid in my mind. It was a painting of a huge landscape with pilgrims leaving their homes and extended families to go overseas. It wasn't the beauty of the painting I remember, but the fact that I stood in front of it with my mom while she read the description to me, tears welling up and spilling over her eyes thinking of those pilgrims leaving their dear friends and families they may never see again. And as I stood there next to her, I realized that art is amazing. It can create something so much bigger than itself, such emotion, such feeling. I think it was right then and there that I realized it: I was in love with art.

As much as I adored art growing up, and even contemplated majoring in it in college, I didn't. I'm not a docent at a famous museum. Instead I'm settled down in the middle of suburbia with five little kids. And really the only "famous" original art works I've seen lately are the ones my kids have made, hung proudly all over our laundry room walls. Some day maybe I'll do more in the fine art field. But for now I'm happy to follow my amazing mother's example and try to let my love rub off on my own kids. I take them to any museum I can. I volunteer to do the "Art Masterpiece" program at the elementary school in each of their classes. I encourage them to paint and draw and sketch whatever they can.

I love art. I love that my kids love it, too.

It's the same with books. Not only did my mother write them, but she read a wealth of wonderful books to us, religiously. There was nothing more soothing to me growing up than the voice of my mother reading us a story. She read us book after book, in airplanes, around campfires, on the intercom in our good old family van. I'm so thankful for how she rubbed off on me. And I hope to rub that love off on my kids as well.

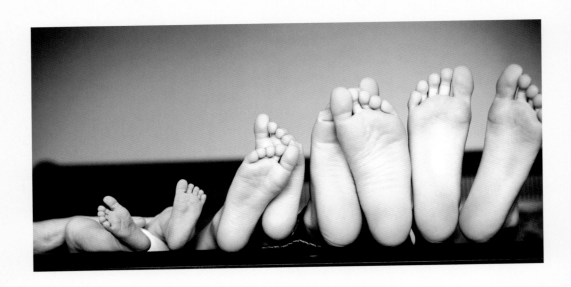

ROOTS

Shawni

We are all part of a big, humongous puzzle. We're made up with parts from many different people—our roots. Our ancestors. We may have inherited a great sense of humor from Uncle Fred, or a passion for travel from Aunt Petunia. We may have bright red hair because our great, great, great-grandfather did, too, and we may have inherited a knack for gardening from our grandmother.

Our children are part of quite a heritage, and I realized recently that my kids don't really get that. They don't know enough stories about their ancestors, or even about me, like I wish they did. If they discover they've got a natural talent for playing the piano, I'd love for them to realize it was probably passed down to them from their great-grandma. When they work hard at their homework, I want them to know that their dad works even harder at work—to provide them with what they need. I want them to know that the bright sparkle in their eyes comes from their Nana. When they come up with imaginative, creative ideas, I want them to know that that was a gift directly from their Grandfather. And when they feel in their hearts that they just need to look out for those who are feeling left out at school, well, that's easy, that gift is from their Grammie.

In wishing for my kids to know more about these wonderful "parts" that make up the pieces they're made of, I realized I have a lot of great material for storytelling. Not only is it interesting, but it's true. It's about me. It's about my grandparents. It's about my parents. And when I tell it in story form my kids love to listen to it.

I told them the one where this little boy and his brother got scared in a hotel room one night because they thought they heard a lion. It turned out to be a man snoring in the next room.

That scared little boy was my dad.

I told them the one where a little girl got to drive a big huge tractor when she was only ten because she lived on a farm, and how her amazing mother taught her to work so hard.

That was my mom, and her mom.

I told them the one about a girl in sixth grade who couldn't close her mouth because she had such big buck teeth to go along with braces and head gear. And how she hated it but she was so glad she went through it when she finally got her braces off.

That was me.

I told them the one about this brave boy, the oldest of five kids, who lost his dad to cancer when he was fifteen. This one makes me cry every time I think about it. His widowed mother was so strong and took care of so much all by herself. And that boy had to kick in and sort of be a dad to his younger siblings at a very young age. Although they both had to go through much heartache, it made them into extraordinary people.

They were my dad and my grandma.

And I can't forget the one about how this very handsome boy took his girlfriend on a hike up to a waterfall. He got really nervous and shaky as he pulled a diamond ring out of his sock (yes, his sock), put it on her finger and asked her to marry him. She said yes with stars in her eyes and knew that her life was going to be one great adventure with this man by her side.

That was Dave and me.

There's nothing like a good story. Especially when it connects our kids to their roots and helps them (and us mothers) put together the puzzle of who they really are. The secret is to share stories of those roots to help them connect the pieces.

TIME

Shawni

There's this saying that the best thing you can give your kids is your time. I have to agree whole-heartedly. When someone gives us a listening ear, is willing to drop other things for us, and is willing to serve us, isn't that one of the best things in the world?

My own parents are amazing examples of giving kids their time.

My dad, for example, started an "interview" tradition when we were young. I'm sure he had many other things on his plate, but he took time to really get to know us—as individuals. It was our time to be set apart from the crowd of our other eight siblings. Interview time was our time. He'd corner us and have a little interview with us. He'd ask all kinds of questions. He'd help us figure out our goals. When we were really little he'd write the initial of our best talents on each of our ten fingertips (I was good at art so he'd write a little *a* for art with a ballpoint pen on my thumb, then move on to my next talent, which he'd add to my index finger). He'd make us feel so great about ourselves. He'd ask what he could help with. And the amazing thing was that when we grew up and moved away he'd still call us for our interviews. Since I was the second child, the second Sunday was mine. He'd call and give me my traditional interview over the phone. My dad's a busy man. I'm sure he's got a million other things going on. But he never hesitates to give us his time.

As I'm sure all parents do, I too try to carve out the gift of time for my kids. Without fail, though, the everyday chaos always seems to gets in the way. One thing I've figured out for now is lunch dates. I know there will be a time when I'll need to take school time more seriously. Soon my kids will be in junior high, and then filling out college applications before I know it. But this is elementary school for crying out loud. Shhh, this is a secret: I let my kids miss some of school sometimes. I take them out to long lunches one by one once a month. It's the only time I could figure out to have more one on one time together. Yes, Lucy and Claire tag along, and yes, sometimes they're enough to upset the good people who thought Wendy's would be a nice quiet break from their work day and don't want to be hampered by two kids throwing French fries around in the air. But that child I took out of school still knows that it's *her* special day, and her eyes sparkle with the excitement of getting to order whatever she wants and having me just concentrate on her. And I love that when it's Max's turn, my big tough boy still begs for it to be "his" day.

I try to follow in my dad's footsteps and have a little interview with each child while we're at lunch. I go through my parents' five facets. We make monthly goals of how they can do better in each of these categories. And then, ideally, I schedule these things on my calendar so I can follow through in helping them (not so good at that yet). I love connecting with my kids. I love telling them I love them over our "gourmet" food.

Another gift of time we've loved giving our kids is what we call "Late Nights." We were much better at this when our kids were all younger and had more similar bedtimes, but we still try to stick with it in when we can. "Late Nights" are when the kids get to rotate each getting a turn once a week to stay up ten or fifteen minutes later than the others. They eat this up. It's such a short amount of time, but they think it's the luckiest thing ever when it's their turn, and we love to give them some undivided one-on-one attention.

One more gift of my time I give my kids is Mother's Day letters. Being the fanatic about record keeping that I am, I love to write letters to my kids. I want them to have a record of how much I adore every little thing they do, written in my own handwriting. When Max and Elle were little I was great at it and I'd write to them all the time. But when it got harder and harder to set aside time to do it, I decided I'd ask for a couple hours alone in my room each Mother's Day so I could write a special love note to each of my kids. I love knowing that I have those compiled for them. I want them to forever remember how much I love them at every stage and what I've noticed about them each year.

Giving our time doesn't need to be a big deal—and even a short minute of time can work wonders. My kids glow when we figure out we both like the same thing, and I take the time to acknowledge that must mean we're in the "club" for liking that particular thing. Every time we have tomatoes, Claire likes to point out that we're in the "tomato club."

The more time we give our kids, the more we understand them. The more we see them as individuals, the better mothers we can be.

PART 5

GIVE OWNERSHIP

. . . it's the solution to most kids' problems

GOALS

Linda

The more that Richard and I speak with parents, the more we realize that one of the greatest secrets of raising successful, responsible children is to give them ownership. As soon as kids become old enough to begin to be accountable for their own actions, parents need to pass over the mantle of ownership. This last section of secrets will address that issue. We cannot emphasize enough how important this concept is to parenting. The more we use this concept in our counseling, the more we realize it is the solution to most kids' problems. Usually we suggest that this transfer of ownership from being a little child to realizing that they can accomplish things on their own happens at about age eight—the age of accountability.

Ownership is key to changing your job description as a parent from taskmaster, referee, and drill sergeant to one of consultant. Unfortunately we didn't figure this out until some of our older children were off to college; but it is an amazing key to turning over the joy of progress to the children. Let me explain how ownership relates to goals.

When our kids were growing up, we gave them each a piece of poster paper at the beginning of each school year and had them use it to plan out their school year. We asked them to figure out their theme for the year—something that they wanted to have in their minds to accomplish that year. For example, one year one of our son's themes was "Step It up a Notch." An illustration to the side of his theme included a foot stepping up on a notch. He knew exactly what that meant to him, which is the first step of success. Then we asked the kids to divide their charts into three sections. The first was to write their academic goals, which could include the grades they wanted to earn in each class or specific things they wanted to learn. The second section was for extracurricular goals. This was about the music lessons they were taking, their athletic goals for basketball or soccer and any clubs they were involved in at school. The third category was for character goals. We asked them to think about goals to improve their empathy for other people, their friendship skills, and issues concerning values like honesty, integrity, self-reliance, and courage to do what is right.

In our wildest dreams we could not have thought of all the things they wrote down to accomplish some years. Some had little circles by each goal (only three or four in each area) so that they could fill them in as they accomplished their goals. Suddenly, instead of us standing over them saying things like, "Have you got you homework done?" "You've really got to work on your defense in basketball!" or "Why can't you be nicer to Amy when she needs your support?" we could instead ask, "What can I do to help you with your goals?" What a paradigm shift! We couldn't believe the difference this ownership of their own goals made in our kids' abilities to take responsibility for their own actions and in our relationships with our children.

Sure there were kids who weren't that motivated in any case and had to be reminded over and over to look at their goals and let us know how they were doing, but you see the value of having that be *their* responsibility, not yours!

In the summer we had a whole different deal. In fact, it was called "Summer Deals." When the kids were too young to have summer jobs but knew that they would have to buy their own school clothes in the fall (see the secret on Money for details), we gave them a way to earn money in the summer by writing the things they wanted to accomplish and then having them make a deal with us parents for a monetary reward for each goal they accomplished. Again, they had ownership of their own goals as they planned how many buckets of tennis balls they wanted to hit, how much piano practice they would do each day, or which piece they wanted to play in a recital at the end of the summer. It included how many books they wanted to read and what particular things they wanted to learn. Each goal was attached to a dollar amount, which went toward buying their school clothes in the fall.

Our youngest daughter, Charity, made a goal chart when she was nine that was priceless! Somehow at that age she was rather obsessed with percentages, which makes her goals pretty humorous. Here is an example of what she wrote:

Get in shape and don't be lazy by 70 percent.

Get only three cavities for the year.

Become 30 percent more interested in others.

Be 60 percent nicer.

Not only will you find your children's goal-setting process fun and entertaining, it will help you see what a difference it makes when your kids feel ownership of their own goals instead of trying to get them to accomplish goals you have set for them. It is an incredible secret to creating a happy, self-motivated child.

ARGUMENTS

Linda

How can I let my kids have ownership of their own arguments?" you might ask. We figured this out after many years of trial and error and a good idea from a friend. With nine kids walking around our house, you could rightly assume that sibling rivalry reigned pretty often in the walls of our home. Figuring out who did what, who should be punished and how severely, became a never-ending battle and an exhausting experience.

Finally in a family meeting we laid out our new system for solving sibling rivalry that went something like this: Okay, Eli and Charity, we want you two to act out the argument you had yesterday for the family. With giggles, they tried to remember what the argument was about and did a pretty good job of ending with shoving and hitting.

Next we announced that from now on, whenever two kids were fighting they would be sent directly to a place called the Repenting Bench. We started with just two chairs placed next to each other and later formalized it when we bought a small pew from an old church in England while we lived there for a few years. It was just big enough for two kids to sit on and was very uncomfortable—not a nice place to sit for very long! We informed the kids that as soon as we heard a fight break out they would be instructed to go to the Repenting Bench and go through a little routine which included first figuring out what they did wrong. Now, if you do this, be warned that some kids will insist that they did absolutely nothing wrong, that the other kid was totally at fault! When this happened in our house, we informed the offending child that it took two to tango and that they could have done something to prevent the argument and they must sit there—on the bench—until they figured out what they did wrong. When they did, they called Richard or me (or even a baby-sitter if you want to go that far) over to tell what they did. When each child had confessed, they were required to say, "I'm sorry. Will you forgive me? I'll try not to do it again" and then they had to give each other a little hug before leaving the bench.

I'm sure there are some questions in your mind about how this actually works. Will the kids actually go to the bench? What if one forgives and the other doesn't? How long do you let them sit there? Isn't that just pretty arbitrary when you know they'll say anything to get off the bench? The answers are different for every family and every situation, but here are some answers that we think are usually right.

First, if you have practiced this little routine in a family meeting and the kids know that this is a new tradition and everyone is in it together, they will normally comply. I will say that it's a little harder to work out if your children are fourteen and fifteen than if they are eight and nine. Good luck on that! But it is fun to actually see them apologize and sincerely say they're sorry, to be able to dissipate the bad feelings and to actually have ownership of the solution to their arguments. You no longer have to be the referee, in which case you are usually wrong and maligned anyway. Just letting them figure it out themselves is a huge step in the ownership arena.

What never occurred to us when we first started this little routine when our kids were small were the long-term effects. We have grown kids now who are all best friends. All those pent-up bad feelings that never get resolved among kids who go through stages of not liking each other usually get nipped in the bud on that repenting bench.

It should also be noted that last year we built a new house and had fun with a real auction where we auctioned off to our adult kids all the household goods we weren't taking with us. We gave them all the same amount of monopoly money and they could bid on whatever they wanted. Our friend who is a professional auctioneer came in with his microphone and the whole bit, and we had a ball watching the big event unfold. Funnily enough, the thing that went for the most money was the Repenting Bench. Noah spent a fortune on it! When Richard asked him why he wanted it so much, he replied, "Dad, I spent half of my life on that thing!"

HARD WORK

Shawni

A while ago I re-read what I have called my favorite book for as long as I can remember—*The Good Earth.* It was my second time through, and because of the different stage I am in my life now, different things caught my attention. But even with a different take on it through my more mature eyes, I can still proclaim it as my favorite. I guess one of the reasons it affected me so much this time around is because I love the correlation it gives between hard work and happiness. To put it simply, when the main character (Wang Lung) is working hard, he is completely fulfilled and satisfied. In my mind he is truly happy. He doesn't have time to feel sorry for himself—he's just so thankful for what he's got. Things around him work together for good. When he's idle and gets caught up in his riches and forgets how working hard on the land makes him whole, things fall apart.

It affected me because it hit close to home. As I work each day to rear my children the best way I can, I long to rear them right, to instill in them good values, and to help them someday become wonderful contributors to society. And as I read my book and contrasted my life to the lives of the characters in *The Good Earth,* I saw a stark contrast. Yes, times have changed. Yes, I'm extremely grateful for modern conveniences and how much easier they make life. But it worried me because it hit me stronger than ever that I'm rearing my kids in an affluent generation where hard work isn't such the norm anymore (at least not where I live).

I often smile to myself as I walk into the gym. I picture my great-great-grandma walking in there with her jaw dropping to the ground, wondering what in the world all these people are doing running around in place and lifting weights. People back then got such a workout from life; they didn't need gyms or double joggers or exercise DVDs. They worked from sunup to sundown and didn't get breaks. And I believe they were strong because of it—not only in body but in mind. Then I think of my own generation when I was a kid (which wasn't *that* long ago). Where I lived, kids had to ride their bikes or walk to get where they needed/wanted to go. They worked to mow their own lawns and had to earn their own money.

Now I watch parents drive their kids everywhere—even down the block (sadly I am not an exception!). I see these kids with wallets full of money given to them, who have time to waste playing video games or watching TV while cleaning ladies dust the furniture around them. What does their future hold? Are we starving them of opportunities to make themselves strong? How will they function as adults if everything is given to them on a silver platter and we shelter them from things that are hard, holding them back from stretching their wings?

I have to back up and say that of course there are so many wonderful examples of hard workers in our day, and so many kids are so darn responsible it makes me drool because I wish my kids were more that way. But it scares me to see the direction society's moving. I know times have changed, and it's scary to let kids roam most neighborhoods on their bikes, and kids are so busy taking classes or with extracurricular activities that they don't have time to clean their own bathrooms, but that makes me sad. I'm not sure how to find the balance.

There are things I want my kids to have—great vacations together as a family, a nice place they can call home, lots of great books to read, classes to boost their coordination, musicality, self-esteem, and so on. But I also want to help them find the joy involved with working hard and to feel the ownership of something they have earned. I want them to have to earn money for a new book or toy they're dying for, to have them walk or ride their bikes to school (even when there's a bus available) and realize how thankful they are for a body that works so well. I want to watch them tear up when they realize they've helped someone who really needed them after they've given selfless service, to feel the full heart that comes with giving up something important because someone else needs it more. I want my children to lose themselves in the joy and satisfaction and feeling of ownership that comes from hard work. The question is, how do I give these, the most important things, to them? How do I make life harder in order to make it better?

I guess the bottom line is that there's nothing like sitting back together after a Saturday's hard work and taking pride in the ownership of how the house smells and looks, and how beautifully manicured the yard is, and realizing that we've done it all ourselves—we've worked so hard and now we can really play. That kind of hard work gives a high that I want my kids (and my husband and me) to have more of.

I believe that teaching kids hard work is the secret that will help them weather the storms they'll no doubt face in life. If we teach them to deal with them by working hard and facing difficulties full-on—taking ownership in what's hard and tackling it—they'll be well-balanced and better for the wear. That's what *The Good Earth* taught me this time around.

CHOICES

Linda

One segment of our seminars with families is about helping kids from ages eight to fourteen make good decisions. We suggest that parents give their children a special journal where they can record their life experiences . . . but that they should first have them turn to the *last page* of that journal and put a title at the top that says, "Decisions I Have Made in Advance."

We then propose that they talk through with their kids in a private, one-on-one session, certain things that they can decide right now. It's fun for kids to think about decisions they *can't* decide right now, such as where they are going to college, who they are going to marry, or where they will live in fifteen years. Then we have them think about the decisions they actually *can* make right now. This would include a discussion about whether they could decide right now to always be honest. Those decisions could also involve a discussion about taking drugs, looking at pornography, smoking, drinking, and early-recreational sex.

We suggest that parents not try to do this all at once, but that they spend several Sunday afternoons talking with their kids about each decision they may want to make. Have children make a decision one at a time and encourage them not to write their decision down until they are sure that it is their own choice.

We ask the parents to present a worst-case scenario for each decision. For example, on deciding about whether or not to be totally honest you might say: "What if you missed a day at school and the next day you found that there is a pop quiz in history. You haven't read the chapter and you know you will fail, but the smartest girl in the room is sitting right across from you with her answers in plain sight. What would you do?" Almost every child will be faced with that dilemma at some point, and if he or she has already thought it through and made the decision to be honest, the answer will be easy for him when it gets to crunch time! When the child has thoughtfully made a decision he or she should write it on the back page of that journal and it should then be formally signed and dated. It becomes a pact with him/herself.

Sometimes, after a day-long seminar, we have the kids join their parents for the last hour. On one occasion, after having an in-depth discussion about making decisions in advance with the kids present, we chose a darling twelve-year-old boy in the audience to be our guinea pig. We asked him about what he felt he could write on his page about decisions he could make in advance. He immediately said, "I will never take drugs." When asked if he was absolutely sure, he said, "Yes, I'm sure." He was ready to write it down, sign, and seal it.

Then we suggested that there might be a time when that decision would become difficult to keep. We told him to project himself forward five years when he might be at a party with a girl he *really* liked and that she might plead with him to try a little white pill she had that everyone at the whole party had tried. We warned him that she might promise it was not really drugs but would make him feel so great and then he would be "one of them." In that case, we asked him what he would say? He smiled and said, "I would just say, 'No, I know that is a drug and I promised myself that I would never take drugs when I was twelve years old. Would you want me to break that promise?'"

Perfect! Having that answer firmly in his mind will be a huge advantage to him as he enters the scary world of teenagers. When we asked him whether or not he could promise himself that he would never cheat on a test in school, he hesitated. It felt as though it was already too late on that one and he'd have to reconsider that before he could write it down. With giggles from the audience, he promised that he would consider that and let us know his answer.

When we really help our kids think through their own decisions, *it gives them ownership of their own goals* rather than hearing you lecture over and over again about the dangers of drugs, alcohol, pornography, and premarital sex. Once *they* make the decisions, they *own* them, and the likelihood of follow through, though not guaranteed, rises significantly. It's a pretty good insurance policy and a grand safety net for your children, who are walking a tightrope into a scary world with whacky values that often don't match with your own beliefs.

Working with our own children on their "Decisions in Advance" has been probably the most effective thing we could have done to give them ownership of their own lives and ability to make good choices. They had answers ready for tough situations. The decision was already made. It has been an anchor in many tough situations that has kept them rooted and helped them dodge many an unexpected bullet in their growing-up years. There is certainly no guarantee that kids will always make the right decisions, but the secret is that if you help kids take ownership for their own choices they're much more likely to follow through. And it's pretty comforting as a parent to know your kids have a plan in mind rather than feeling like you are sending them off into an often valueless world in a little boat headed for Niagara Falls without an oar or an anchor and yelling, "Good Luck!"

MONEY

Linda

Long before your child goes off to college with a credit card, one of the best things you can teach him is how to deal with money. Money has been called the root of all evil but it can also be the root of all (well . . . *lots*) of happiness. Richard and I have written books about the importance of teaching kids how to deal with money (you can find new and used copies of *Teaching Children Responsibility* and *Three Steps to a Strong Family* on Amazon and Barnes and Noble online for almost nothing if you want detailed information).

In a nutshell, we have found that money is the perfect vehicle to teach kids beginning when they are seven or eight how to feel ownership, how to save for a future cause, how to feel delayed gratification, how to spend wisely, save carefully, and how to give to others. We decided early on that giving our kids an allowance was just teaching them how to stand in the dole line for a handout each week. We wanted them to earn it! We wanted them to feel ownership for it.

Because Richard was raised doing a paper route for money and I was raised practicing violin and piano for my money (my mom insisted that I buy my own clothes from age eight and doubled my money if I practiced consistently all week), we had been taught the value of money at early ages. We tried the paper route for a couple of years with a couple of our boys and their siblings helped with those on occasion, but we soon realized that we were not going the way of the paper route forever, even though we admire those who do!

We devised a way to have the kids earn their money with four pegs (a star chart or stickers will work just as well) that they were required to put in each day to accomplish their daily goals. The first peg was plugged in when they finished their morning jobs: bed made, teeth brushed, homework ready to go. The second peg represented their job/zone. It was plugged in when they completed clearing an area of the house they were in charge of keeping clean every day: the front hall, a closet, etc. The third peg was for their practicing and homework, and the fourth was the nighttime peg that they put in when they had laid out their clothes for the next day, said their prayers, and brushed their teeth. At the end of the day they put a post-it note in a box that has been initialed by one of the parents at the child's request without a reminder. The note (or "slip") would have a 1, 2, 3, or 4 on it, which translated into different amounts of money on "payday" at the end of the week. If they forgot their "slip," it was a good lesson in consequences when they had no money to spend that week. The kids soon realized when they went on "the system" that putting those pegs in every week was important because from the time they were eight years old, they were allowed/required to buy their own clothes and all their "I wants." No signed slips equaled no money. Consistency on all five weekdays was rewarded with money doubled.

There are so many details involved in this system that you will need a more thorough explanation to make it work (see *Three Steps to a Strong Family* for a more in-depth description of "the system"), but the bottom line for the purposes of this book is to say that it did change the initiative for our kids. Instead of them begging us for things at the store that we didn't want to buy for them, on this system when they asked for things, we could say, "Sure you can have that. Did you bring your checkbook?"

Instead of pestering them all day about doing their jobs, they either did them or not and got the reward or not. The initiative was completely theirs. The kids came up with ingenious ideas to make things work. After being frustrated about forgetting to put his slips in the box over and over again, Talmadge decided to put a rock under his pillow so that when his head hit the rock every night, it would remind him to get up and put that slip in the box.

Richard, who had always wanted to be a banker, called the children in to the kitchen table on Saturday morning for "payday," where they got what they deserved from their work that week. It was a great time to praise those who did well and ignore those who didn't. We could almost hear those slackers mutter under their breath, "Next week, I'm going to do better!"

Sure there were some kids who were more motivated than others. Some I took shopping at Nordstrom and some to Deseret Industries for their school clothes. Some, who didn't care one whit about clothes, got motivated when a need for electronic equipment and games became a passion. Even though most of our children have become amazingly financially responsible, we all still laugh about one whose money burns a great big hole in her pocket and she just can't quite seem to "get it." Some are naturally conservative with money (we have two that are painfully so), others really had to work with the consequences of bad choices, which is exactly what we wanted. It is so much better for kids to struggle with those issues when they are ten instead of when they take off for college with a credit card.

We also had a system for giving. Ten percent for tithing for the Church (or more if they wanted to give to a specific cause). Twenty percent was designated for savings, with large interest incentives for their college educations. And the other 70 percent was all theirs.

Certainly there are a thousand ways to work with money and kids. One friend has a wonderful Web site at activeallowance.com that has a simple way to put these systems on paper. One dad, who was a contractor, gathers his kids to the kitchen table on Saturday mornings where there is a job list (prepared by the mom). He has them bid for the jobs by sealed bid! The ones who want to buy a new prom dress or are working for new skis will do almost anything at almost any price to earn it! The important thing is that the kids perceive their money as their own. Suddenly they start hanging up their shirts that they paid $29.95 for, and in our family, it was never hand-me-downs, but sell-me-downs!

Turn the ownership of your kids' needs and wants over to them and see what happens.

It requires time and effort and consistency, but it works like an infrastructure that in the long run will save you time, hassle, and headaches as your children perceive ownership and responsibility for their own things. The secret is to keep it light and have fun!

CLEANING

Shawni

As mothers we are on a continual quest for cleanliness. Not only do we want to keep our homes clean and organized, but we want to teach our kids to pitch in and to value the importance of cleanliness. Not just now when they live with us, but down the road when they have their own homes. If we can give them ownership of their own cleaning, wow! what a difference it makes.

As I'm sure all mothers do, I have tried over and over again to make cleaning and organization "plans" involving my kids as key contributors. My husband and I have tried everything from singing the Barney clean-up song to inspire little kids to lend a hand to paying the kids a nickel or dime for everything they can pick up and put away. We've tried making up elaborate sticker charts, structuring a system for each child to be in charge of cleaning particular "zones" in the house, and we've even tried not letting kids come out of their messy rooms until they're clean. You name it, we've tried it. Some things work better than others.

I think each family has to struggle to come up with the best solution to the continual cleaning saga for their own family, but I wanted to share a couple of my favorite ideas:

Clean Ten. I have no idea where I heard this, but I love it. (Thank you, you wise mother out there who made this up!) Whenever things get really cluttery around our house I just say, "clean ten," and the kids have to each pick up and put away ten things. I love it because they've been trained pretty well by now, and the response is pretty much automatic. Not only does it help to get the house clean quick, but it helps the kids know where everything really goes so they can be better at putting things away in the first place.

Job Charts. Yes, everyone has a different version. But the key is to *have* them. We started the job process years ago by just telling each child their household chores. It didn't work. Kids need something tangible. They want to see what they need to do and cross it off when they're done. So one Saturday, instead of just telling the kids what they needed to do (and arguing with them all day about how they better get on it), I printed them each a copy of their own particular Saturday chores. I put a little circle next to each job for them to color in when they were done. Man oh man, I couldn't believe the difference. They were begging for their job charts every Saturday (they know they can't play with friends until all those circles are colored in). I had to kind of smile that I could really put any job on the planet on there and they didn't complain—just as long as each child's list was reasonably equal. Something about the coloring in the circles worked a few magic tricks . . . and still does.

Cleaning Fairy. It's amazing that jobs can become miraculously more fun when you're doing them as a service for someone else. Sometimes when Claire and I realize a brother or sister has forgotten to do a job before they left for school (which means no playing with friends after school), we sprinkle "magic invisible fairy dust" on ourselves and turn into "cleaning fairies" who do the jobs that were left undone. When the school kids come home asking to play with a friend and I ask the dreaded question—"Did you do your morning jobs?"—Claire and I look at each other in delight when we see their devastation turn to surprise when they realize they forgot, but that someone else did it for them. Claire and I pretend to be completely puzzled as to how the jobs got done, and the older kids get to go off and play with a knowing smile. They know someone helped them out. And that makes their day.

Make Cleaning Fun. It's important not to just be the taskmaster of drudgery when you're trying to get your kids involved in cleaning. You need to make it fun. In our house when we really

want to get things clean in a hurry, we turn on some rocking music full blast, turn on a timer to see how fast we can do it, and go for it. It does wonders for making kids more excited about cleaning.

Pick Your Battles. If I had my kids clean the playroom every day I think all of us would go crazy. I've realized that, at least in our house, as long as it gets a thorough cleaning every Saturday, I'm not going to worry about it the rest of the week. I let my kids play and use their imaginations to their hearts' content the other days of the week. I also decided that the kids need a break once in a while, and announced to them one night a while ago that Sunday would be our no-bed-making day. I almost laughed out loud when I watched their jaws drop as they looked at me in complete awe and admiration. They love Sunday messy bed day.

So the secret is to hand over the ownership of cleaning! Even really young kids can understand that it's their responsibility to get certain things done before they can do something fun—even if it's just something as little as making sure that they put their beloved blankie behind their pillow each morning or help put away the silverware from the dishwasher. And sometimes I think we underestimate how much big kids can do to help out. They can be the best cleaners. The secret is really taking out enough time to teach them "how" to do it. But if we put in the time and give them ownership of their particular jobs, it's amazing to watch them take off from there.

THE BIG TALK

Linda

One of the most fun things we have done with our kids that also just happens to be one of the biggest secrets in creating a healthy sense of the wonder and the special nature of sex is to have an early, positive pre-emptive "strike." Although maturity levels, location, and media issues are different for each family, we have found that the perfect age to begin the initial "big talk" is age eight.

About a month before our kids turned eight we started saying, "Hey, guess what? On your birthday Dad and I are going to take you out to your favorite restaurant and then we are going to tell you about the most wonderful, awesome, miraculous thing in the whole world. We're not going to tell you what it is until then but you just won't believe how interesting it will be! We can't wait!" Every week until the big night we would remind them about how excited we are for the birthday when they could learn about one of the most incredible and amazing things on earth. "It's about you," we would say, "but we're not going to tell you any details until we have our talk."

I must admit that when we were at the door ready to take our first daughter to dinner and "the talk," I looked at Richard and said, "You know, honey, you are so good at explaining things, why don't you just do this on your own and let me know how it goes." He grabbed my hand with a grin and said, "We can't lose if there's one of us on each side of her." And we were off. We took them to their favorite restaurant and then sometimes retired to another private place where we had the talk. The older kids claim that we had the talk right at the restaurant. Whatever works!

We took a book with us that explained things on an eight-year-old level. The illustrations were sort of humorous, which kept things light, and the child could actually read one page and we would read the next. It was called *Where Did I Come From* by Peter Mayle, and though I have had parents say there is a page or two they "razor-bladed" out, it does give a good explanation of what actually happens. Other books are probably even better now (and probably some are scary and worse)!

At the end of the book, we asked them whether they had heard anything about that before. Maybe we have very naive children, but they all claimed that they hadn't. Even if they had heard some of the words, they hadn't put things together. When we asked for questions, we must admit there were some pretty funny ones. At the end of each discussion we made it a point to ask, "When something is that special, would you want to save it for someone you loved and were totally committed to?" Their answer was always an emphatic "Yes!"

We had so much fun with it that Richard and I wrote a whole book on the subject called *How to Talk to Your Child about Sex.* It includes not only how to answer young children's questions up until the "Big Talk," but it also has sample dialogues of exactly what to say on that special night. It includes what your child would probably say and how to respond to that. It was so popular that we actually put the dialogue on our Web site at valuesparenting.com. (Click on "How to Talk to Your Child About Sex" on the homepage.)

[Note from Shawni: Don't try this talk without this dialogue handy. It's great to have something all written out for you to reference while trying to keep your composure.]

Of course "The Big Talk" is hopefully only the beginning of an open dialogue that will ensue as your children come up with questions as they mature. In the book we also present topics of discussion for adolescents and teenagers that will bring out their feelings about one of the most important topics they will encounter. It gives your child a very positive approach to the most intimate relationship on earth. From then on, when you see something objectionable on television (which pops up almost every other minute), you can sit by your child and explain how you feel about making sex seem so trite and easily accessible. What you are doing as you teach is to make your child a critic of what they are seeing. They can learn how to reject the perverted notions of the media, which is important because you are not always going to be sitting by that child as they venture into a very promiscuous world.

That talk will give your child ownership of the knowledge that sex is a wonderful part of life to be enjoyed with one special person at an appropriate time and place. Instead of scaring kids about the dangers of sex, which they will get enough of at school and from friends, you will be teaching them that in its proper setting it is one of the most amazing and incredible experiences of life. After all it brought them to this world, and it will enable them to someday bring children to their own family.

We can promise that as hard as it is and no matter what happens, you'll always be glad you did it. Our son Noah, a student and married for only about eighteen months, called one night from college to say that he and Kristi wanted to meet us for dinner at his favorite restaurant downtown. When we got there, he insisted on sitting at a specific table. After enjoying the food, he got a twinkle in his eye and said that he and Kristi wanted to show us something. She pulled out a pregnancy stick that showed a positive result, and we were ecstatic! Then he asked us if we remembered that very table was where we sat when we had "The Big Talk."

Payday!

SERVICE

Linda

After years of dreading facing the hassle of the Christmas season for the umpteenth time, we figured out how to make Christmas new again. For those of you with small children, I must say that for many years you have to pay your dues to Santa Claus before you'll be able to try what I am about to suggest in this secret. How well I remember those Christmases spent desperately trying to be Santa's helper and fill those short but numerous lists of Christmas wishes from our nine young children. While visions of playing with shiny red train sets and actually feeding Baby Alive with a spoon danced through Josh and Shawni's heads, I was out there beating the pavement, trying to find a train in red and being horrified that, after a two-hour wait in a line for Shawni's Baby Alive, the mother just in front of me got the very last doll, and I was going to have to tell Shawni that Baby Alive was dead!

One year Richard and I decided that we were just too saturated with "stuff" to pack in another load for Christmas. Although there were still a lot of things that the kids wanted, we decided to propose something that we hoped they would desire even more.

At a family meeting in October, before they started thinking about what they might want for Christmas that year, we gave them a choice. They could have another Christmas, just like the others with them giving and receiving stuff that they would most likely soon forget, or we could buy each of them a ticket to Bolivia, where we could do a service project for a little village on the Altiplano, in the Andes Mountains, 14,000 feet above sea level. The project was to dig trenches for PVC pipes that water would run through from a cistern on the mountainside, already installed by another humanitarian group the year before. The goal would be to get water running through those pipes and into the village by New Year's Eve. We told them it would be hard work with picks and shovels and that there would no Christmas presents for them—just the joy of bringing the gift of water to the people of a village that had never had running water.

The older kids were delighted by the idea, but our youngest, who was eleven, had to think about it for a day or two. Giving up those coveted gifts wasn't easy, but she succumbed with the thought of sharing her Christmas with kids who were desperately in need.

I could write a book about our week with those incredible villagers. Several other American families were with us and we, along with the sweet villagers, all immediately became fast friends. Some of the younger parents and children spoke Spanish, but most of the villagers spoke an Indian dialect that only our leader could understand. Despite the language barrier, we quickly learned that it couldn't stop kids communicating with kids. They had fun dancing together at night to the live Bolivian band that played and showing each other how to make crafts.

The villagers worked side by side with us every day and directed the project. For a week we dug trenches in rock-hard dirt with picks and shovels beside little grandmas who worked circles around us, even our big boys, because we were having a very difficult time breathing at 14,000 feet! The villagers were dubious about the plan to have water come down the mountain through the PVC pipe because some of the terrain was uphill and they couldn't imagine that the water could make it to their village.

The American kids didn't complain much about the "different" food, which was well prepared. We were so grateful to have purified water provided for everyone, as well as use of the new latrines (squatters) that the village workers had also built especially for us. The carnival we organized near the end of our expedition was a delight as we saw our kids enjoying the light in the eyes of the little Bolivian children as they went to the fish pond and other booths and were bedazzled by the balloons and stickers, construction paper and markers that we had brought from home for prizes.

But the real payday was on New Year's Eve when, with great ceremony, the village leaders turned on the first tap ever in their village to produce running water. The villagers were amazed and delighted, but the looks on our kids' faces were *priceless!*

For about the same amount of money we would have spent on another Christmas at home, or even taking the kids to Disneyland for a week, we had the wonderful blessing of changing the lives of these beautiful Bolivian people forever, which also happened to change the lives of our own children forever as well!

Children should be at least ten or eleven to go on one of these expeditions, so if you've still got tiny ones, put it on the back shelf as a possibility for the future. But if your children are older and you too are sick of the "stuff" and materialism, make next year's Christmas season new again (contact ascendalliance.org for expedition schedules and countries).

Though a trip like that may not be possible for many, you should know that the next Christmas we found a family within two miles of our house who, although in a different way, were in as great a need as those families we grew to love on the Altiplano with dirt floors and no electricity. We found great joy in fulfilling some of their material needs and hopefully some emotional ones as well.

The outpouring of love and service to others at Christmastime is heartwarming no matter where you live or what your circumstances. The real secret is to find someone your children can help (whether at Christmastime or not) and help them feel ownership in giving from the heart. Let them earn money for a Sub-for-Santa family instead of providing it all yourself. There are hundreds of ideas for service if you seek for them. In the end, service is the greatest secret to unlock many things that families need to learn. It helps us all to become more like the greatest humanitarian who ever lived, who we honor with our service—our beloved Savior Jesus Christ.

POSTSCRIPT

We have loved exploring these secrets with you! As mentioned in our introduction, we know you have secrets of your own that you might want to share. We have partnered with a great interactive Web site called The Power of Moms (www.PowerofMoms.com). There you will find a special section where you can share your own uplifting motherhood ideas or "secrets" for other mothers to enjoy. Additional secrets from us, not included in this book, are also there to get your juices going.

To find information on how to set up a great mothers' group or hold your own CareerMothers Seminar go to www.CareerMothers.com or www.PowerofMoms.com. There you will also find links to the Eyres' Web site, www.valuesparenting.com, and Shawni's blog, 71toes.blogspot.com.

The internet is such a powerful tool in helping us learn and share. We invite you to join us!
—Linda and Shawni

SOURCES CITED

Chicken Soup for the Working Woman's Soul. Edited by Jack Canfield, Mark Victor Hansen, Patty Aubrey, Chrissy and Mark Donnelly. Deerfield, Fla: Health Communications, Inc., 2003.

Eyre, Linda J., et al. *An Emotional First-Aid Kit for Mothers.* SLC: Bookcraft, 1997.

Hugo, Victor. http://quoteworld.org/quotes/6891.

Kimball, Spencer W. *Faith Precedes the Miracle.* SLC: Deseret Book, 1972.

Krasnow, Iris. *Surrendering to Motherhood: Losing Your Mind, Finding Your Soul.* NY: Hyperion, 1997.

Lewis, C. S. *The Collected Letters of C. S. Lewis, Vol. III: Narnia, Cambridge and Joy, 1950–1963.* Edited by Walter Hooper. NY: HarperCollins, 2007.

Lindbergh, Anne Morrow. *Gift from the Sea.* NY: Pantheon Books, 1955.

Okazaki, Chieko N. "Lighten Up!" in *Women and Christ: Living the Abundant Life: Talks Selected from the 1992 Women's Conference Sponsored by Brigham Young University and the Relief Society.* Edited by Dawn Hall Anderson, Susette Fletcher Green, and Marie Cornwall. SLC: Deseret Book, 1993.

Quindlen, Anna. *Loud and Clear.* NY: Ballantine Books, 2004.

Twain, Mark. http://quotationsbook.com/quote/27403/.

ACKNOWLEDGMENTS

For our husbands, who not only encouraged us but sent us away to work. For our children, who allowed us to use their names for good and for ill, and who taught us the true meaning of unconditional love. For the fellow mothers in our family, who added insights and good judgment. For Jana Erickson at Deseret Book, whose optimism inspired us to "get it done."

And for all those amazing mothers who are in the trenches making a difference in the world, one child at a time.

We are forever grateful.